Wrestling
with god

Wrestling
with god

Dr. John Wynn

eGenco

Publisher – eGenCo

Generation Culture Transformation
Specializing in publishing for generation culture change

eGenCo. LLC
824 Tallow Hill Road
Chambersburg, PA- 17202, USA
Phone: 717-461-3436
email: info@egen.co
Website: www.egen.co
            www.goingebook.com

 facebook.com/egenbooks

 youtube.com/egenpub

egen.co/blog

Publisher's Cataloging-in-Publication Data
Wynn, John
        Wrestling with god. A life changing match/John Wynn;
        p.cm.
        ISBN: 978-1-936554-29-4 paperback
              978-1-936554-31-7 ebook
              978-1-936554-32-4 ebook
        1. Religion. 2. Christian life. 3. Enlightenment I. Title
                        203934906

Cover design, interior layout design by Kevin Lepp, kmlstudio.com.

Photography by selenajphotography.com.

For Conferences and Speaking Engagements please contact:
 • email: wrestlingwithgodbook@gmail.com
 • website: www.doctorjohnwynn.com
 • facebook.com/drjohnwynn
 • youtube.com/user/elderwjwynn01

DEDICATION

I want to dedicate this book to my lovely wife Edith. Thank you for being a gentle and kind woman of faith who prays for me daily. You put your dreams on hold to ensure my visions came to pass. I want you to know that the sacrifices you have made for me and our children have not gone unnoticed and that your work and labor of love for the ministry is not in vain. Thank you for exploring this journey with me for the past twenty two years. The best is yet to come. I love you.

I also dedicate this book to my wonderful children: Essence, William John II, Jeremiah, Alexander, Farrah, Josiah, Angelique and Charne'. Over the years we have encountered some very difficult and challenging experiences, but in the midst of them all, each of you stepped up to the plate and hit the ball right out of the park. Thank you for helping Mom and me; we made it through because of your perseverance and support. I want you all to know that I love you and that I am proud of what the Lord is doing in your lives. I speak the blessings of the Lord into your future. Thank you for your endurance and your love.

I give special thanks to my mother, Rochelle Wynn, and to all of my sisters: Patricia, Robbye, Leisa, Karen, Wilhelmenia, Juanita, and Sharon, and to your husbands and families for your continued prayer and support, I love you all. This book is also dedicated in loving memory of my father, the Late Rev. Willie J. Wynn and to my little sister, the Late Rachel Wynn. I love you both and we will never forget you. Special thanks to all my family and friends; Bishops, Superintendents, Pastors, Evangelists and your families for your love and support of my family through the years and during my recovery. Thank you for all your cards, love gifts, visits and telephone calls. I am forever grateful. May the Lord bless you in all your endeavors.

ENDORSEMENTS

In this inspiring and thought-provoking biography, Bishop John Wynn proves that he is a winner in life, though he once believed that everyone else was more loved by God than he. This heart-wrenching, straight-talking, common-sense book should be mandatory reading for all families, and black male adolescents, especially those in single-parent households. Bishop Wynn captures the heart and mind of the reader as he tangos with life's ups and downs, involving self, family, community and church relationships. His quizzical and doubtful mind, battles the deep-rooted love and obedience instilled in him by the early and sudden death of his father—a beloved community leader and pastor. Wynn finally feels victory after wrestling with the gods of vogue as he looks up to the one and only God in heaven and hears the official call. This book beckons the "Hollywood" call.

Dr. Debra Feemster, Education Consultant
Local NAACP Education Chair, Reno, Nevada

After reviewing this masterful work of pastoral transparency, Bishop John Wynn has created an expose' of his personal struggles in mastering the art of husbandry, parenting, pastoral leadership and living out the infused vision given to him by our Lord and Savior Jesus Christ. Very few men of God have attempted to be as open, yet as candid, concerning their passion for the pursuit of pastoral excellence. I have truly been inspired son. You are a Mighty Man of God.

Rev. Glenn E. Taylor, Sr., Senior Pastor,
Greater Light Christian Center, Reno, Nevada

"Wrestling with God" is an extraordinary journey in a Bishop's journey from effectiveness to greatness in his relentless, resilient quest to Experience God. Today there are so many people, youth and young adult, struggling Christians, those who want a closer walk, who have questions and are curious to really know God. Bishop John Wynn takes you from the valley to the mountain, from the inner man, to the outer man, to revolutionize and reenergize his relationship with God. This book touches the heart set, the mindset, the skill set, and the spirit set of your emotions as you read a young man reaching, climbing and marching towards a stronger relationship with God. I highly recommend this book for those who have a commitment to grow and learn in their faith. I am humbled and awed by how Bishop Wynn's story touched my Spirit Man. This anointed man of God has allowed himself to decrease and allowed the Father to increase in the word through his life. This Truth in his life sets him free. A MUST READ!!

Lt. Colonel Ondry Berry, Owner
Guardian Quest, Reno, Nevada

Get ready for a life changing message as John Wynn illustrates though this book how to STOP wrestling with little gods that have taken the focus off of the ALMIGHTY GOD. Through this engaging book you can now with confidence take the Word of God and confront life issues. The author's personal journey provides unique insights that makes this book a must read which can be quickly understood by everyone who desires to experience the importance of building a strong foundation for your family, ministry, career, business, and relationships.

Dr. Ronald C. Hill, Senior Pastor
Love and Unity Christian Fellowship, Compton, CA

C O N T E N T S

INTRODUCTION

Life is full of surprises; some are good and you are excited to embrace them, while others are not so inviting. I recently learned that my life was not just full of surprises; I was actually experiencing wrestling matches in my consciousness. All of my life experiences, unknown to me at the time, were wrestling matches with "little gods" that I created when I took my focus off of "Almighty God". Throughout this book please take note that when not referring to Almighty God, the word "god" is not capitalized. We choose not to acknowledge them, even to the point of violating grammatical rules.

The little gods I created were the gods of uncertainty, insecurity, pain, pride, lust, greed, status, doubt, fear, sickness, misunderstanding and worry. These wrestling matches affected my success in every area of life. This book will illustrate my journey as a husband, father, pastor, community leader and entrepreneur.

Eventually, I learned how to overcome the little gods that I continuously put higher than Almighty God. I will share the encounter with God that I experienced after I broke my left femur and the revelations I received through the Word of God that brought healing to my mind, body and spirit.

Written for leaders in business and ministry as well as those who are trying to achieve their goals and dreams while staying focused on God, this book will empower you to discover the greatness that lies within you!

This is the great confidence that believers have in God: If the Lord is my shepherd, my feeder, I may conclude that I shall not want for anything that is really necessary and good for me. I shall be supplied with whatever I need. However, if I do not have everything I desire, I conclude either that it is not fit or good for me, or that I shall have it in due time.

> *The Lord is my shepherd; I shall not want. He maketh*
> *me to lie down in green pastures: he leadeth me beside the*
> *still waters. He restoreth my soul: he leadeth me in the paths*
> *of righteousness for his name's sake. Yea, though I walk*
> *through the valley of the shadow of death, I will fear no evil:*
> *for thou art with me; thy rod and thy staff they comfort me.*
> *Thou preparest a table before me in the presence of mine*
> *enemies: thou anointest my head with oil; my cup runneth*
> *over. Surely goodness and mercy shall follow me all the days*
> *of my life: and I will dwell in the house of the Lord forever.*
> (Psalms 23:1-6)

I have encountered many experiences in my life that allowed me to understand that the Lord is my shepherd, as well as helped me to identify who God is to me. Below is the definition of who I truly believe Almighty God to be.

Who Is God?

A college essay by Bishop John Wynn, age 24, December 1994

"Who Is God?"

In a world where there are so many opinions about God, I believe it is my duty to argue how the Hebrews view and how I view who God is. The Bible, the world's top best-seller to date, tells a historical story exampling the El Shaddai, the Yahweh and the Jehovah. I will explore these names in different perspectives.

We can't know all about mysterious word "God" until we know more about God. And we can't know all of what the word God means until we go to the language from which the word God is translated; the language of which is the first written record of the revelation of God; the language in which God spoke to Moses and the prophets, which was the Hebrew language.

Missionaries and translators have always had difficulty in finding a suitable word for the Hebrew word we translate God. Those who have attempted to translate this word into Chinese, for instance, have always been divided and still are as to which word is best. One of the greatest of these translations preferred a word which means "Lord of Heaven."

Now a name in the Old Testament was often an indication of a person's character or of some peculiar quality. What one name could be adequate to encompass God's greatness? After all, as one writer declares, a name imposes some limitations. It means that an object or person is this and not that, is here and not there. And if the Heavens cannot contain God, how can a name describe Him?

It is much more rational to believe that the great and infinite and eternal God has given us these different names to express different aspects of God's being and the different relationships God sustains to His character.

The Hebrew names Elohim, translated God in our Bibles; Jehovah, translated LORD; and El-Shaddai, translated God Almighty or Almighty God, relate to the Person of God; the power and glory of His being in Elohim; the expression of Himself as a "God" of righteousness, holiness, love and redemption in Jehovah; and as a Bestower of powers, gifts, blessings and fruitfulness for service, in El-Shaddai.

Most of the names of God arose out of some historical incident and portrayed Jehovah and some aspects of God's character as meeting human needs. The historic incident out of which the name Jehovah Jireh arises is one of the most moving and sufficient in the word of God. It is the story of the last and greatest crisis in the life of Abraham. Every event in Abraham's life led up to this supreme hour, from the time of his call to a high destiny, through every vicissitude, through every joy, through every trial of failure, through every measure of success and blessings, through every hope, promise and assurance.

Jehovah Jireh is translated "the Lord will provide." The name arose out of the incident of Jehovah's provision of a substitute in place of Isaac, who He had commanded Abraham to sacrifice upon the altar. It stands for Jehovah's great provision for man's redemption in the sacrifice of God's only begotten Son, Jesus Christ, the Lamb of God who takes away the sin of the world.

Jehovah Nissi is translated "the Lord our banner" or victory. Moses standing upon the hill with uplifted hands has generally been thought of as interceding with God for the vindication of God's cause in the victory of his people.

Jehovah Shalom is translated "the Lord our peace." God in His own Person is perfect peace. This God must be if He is to be the source of peace to mankind. God is grieved at the sin and corruption of the world, which at creation He had pronounced so good. God is stirred to wrath at the evil of the wicked. God is not indifferent to the sorrows and needs of His people.

Jehovah Rohi is translated "the Lord is my Shepherd." The wonderful grace of God as expressed by the title Shepherd is that God can condescend to such a relationship with mortal, sinful creatures whom He has redeemed.

Jehovah Sidkenu is translated "the Lord our righteousness." How was this righteousness of Jehovah to be applied to men? The spiritually-minded of the Old Testament dispensation clearly understood, on the one hand, that the penalty of death which his sin had incurred must be borne by an innocent sufferer and, on the other, that the innocence or righteousness of the sufferer must be applied to him. It is only on this basis God could declare the guilty innocent and the unrighteous righteous.

Jehovah Rophe is translated "the Lord heals." The Old Testament reveals a number of instances in which God's powers are manifested, even through natural means, to heal the bodies of men. A notable instance is King Hezekiah, who was not only healed but granted a definite additional span of years to his life. Nothing is more obvious, tragic and costly than the toll which sickness has exacted from human life and happiness. I am so glad God is all powerful. God controls both life and death. God is the Essence of our very being. God is the Essence of the world. It was

God who put the stars in the sky. For without God nothing would have been made that was made.

In the Bible, the Apostle Paul confronts the philosophers on Mars Hill, saying, *"God…made the world (cosmos) and all things therein…"* (Acts 17:24), and by this very fact is constituted possessor and ruler of Heaven and Earth, whose presence cannot be confined by space, whose power does not need man's aid, for through God's great will, power and agency all things and nations have their very being.

God does not reside in man-made buildings. I believe God lives in heaven and God lives in the regenerated hearts of man. Although no one has ever seen God, He reveals himself through Christ. The only way you can really know God, is by having a personal encounter with God. Like Moses and the prophets, I have experienced the seen and the unseen things of God, and by this I know for myself that God is the true and living God, the Almighty God, Lord of Lords. God is the only wise God, my Savior.

I have seen God be my Provider; God has provided my every need with food and clothes, with shelter and transportation. He is my Healer; God healed me when I was sick and weak in my body. God is my Refuge; He has been my safety. God is my Help in the very time of trouble. He is my Protector; God protects me from all hurt, harm and danger. God is my Friend; God has been there for me when I could find no one else. God is my Counselor; He speaks to my psyche (soul). God is my Deliverer; He has brought me out of some very difficult situations in my life.

A question was asked, "What sort of cave have I been in?" One cave is known to mankind as the cave of ignorance; the only way you can be set free from this cave is by having a personal encounter with God. In my cave I was full of fear, alone and heartbroken. I had no confidence, joy or peace. In my cave I was distressed, confused, sad and lonely. In my cave I was bound with the chains of bondage. Fear was the strength of my chains, and ignorance was the darkness of my cave.

When I thought about the state of mind I was in, I wondered if God could help me out of my situation. As I prayed to God, He allowed me to recognize that love was the freedom from my chains and that knowledge would give me light in my cave. It was then that I realized that God is love and has all knowledge to understand where to put light in my cave of darkness.

Evelyn Underwood wrote about the language of the heart, the true self, the true lover and the true home. She believed that the true lover was one who knows everything about us and loves us for who we are regardless of our faults. God is my true Lover, who knows everything about me. God is all-loving, God is all-caring, and God is my all in all.

God is described as the Alpha and Omega, the beginning and the end. God is the reason for my knowing who I am. God gave me life, God gave me power, and God gave me the determination to help free others from the chains and caves of life. When I think about God, I think of God's wisdom and I think of God's divine presence.

God is the controller of the cosmos. God is the controller of life, death, and hell, and He is a controller of the grave. God is the energy of our thoughts. God is the Great I AM.

CHAPTER 1

WOUNDED BY CIRCUMSTANCES

In the winter of 1995 I pioneered a new non-profit called Tabernacle of Praise Center. I was so excited. I believed it was going to be an awesome place of worship and training. My wife Edith and I began to look for a building for the newly formed non-profit.

Years earlier, I had a vision that I would have a building that would be large enough to educate, develop and mentor people. After I had the vision, one day I was driving and saw the corner of 65th and Sky Parkway in Sacramento, California. For years I never understood why, but when we began looking for a building for our newly-formed church, I told Edith I wanted to go to the same corner where I had my vision to see if there was a building available.

When we drove up to the corner, there, to our amazement, was a 10,000 square foot empty building, previously Oshman's Sports. I called the number in the window and spoke directly with one of the Oshman Brothers who owned the building. I told him what we wanted to do in the community and he offered to fly from St. Louis to meet with us.

We met Mr. Oshman at Denny's on Florin Road on Martin Luther King Jr. Day. At the time, my family comprised the total membership of the church: Edith and I and our four young children. The non-profit was so new that I had not even opened a checking account yet. I was only twenty-five years old, but I had great faith in God. I realized that if greatness knows no limits, surely I could not put any limits on my Great God.

Mr. Oshman was so impressed with my vision of this new place of worship and training facility that he offered to give us the first and last month's lease payment to make it happen. The lease was $10,000 per month. He gave me the keys to the building and flew back to St. Louis, Missouri, allowing me a couple of weeks to make a decision.

In the meantime, I went into the building along with Edith, my sisters and my family. We sang songs and I prayed to know the will of God. Remember, I hadn't actually started the non-profit yet and had no supporters except my family; therefore, I had no finances to afford a building of this magnitude. However, it was an awesome experience praying in the facility for a while. It actually increased my faith.

My heart was in the right place but I realized it was not yet time. Even if I considered leasing the building, the work that needed to be done would not be ready for our grand opening date. In a situation like this, a man would consult his father, but my father was gone. He had passed away when I was just fifteen and it tore me apart. Now I was a twenty-five year old man with passion but no direction. I imagined my father's voice in my head saying, "Stay focused and keep the faith."

I returned the keys, still wondering why I had the vision of that corner. I also remembered the voice of my father and kept my focus. We continued to witness to the residents in that area. I would park my car in the parking lot of the building and we would hit the streets, trying to change the lives of low-income families in the south side of Sacramento that were struggling, by giving them hope and encouragement. During the holiday season we even gave the families care packages to let them know that we loved them.

I remember the day of the Grand Opening like it was yesterday: February 5, 1995. The event was held at the South Point Inn Hotel on 47th Street, not far from the building we originally looked at. The place was filled to capacity with 500 friends and family. It was a mixed group of well-wishers as well as doubters. The time had come for me to lead the community that I felt God had called me to.

The event was great. People were blessed, the music was awesome. The praise from the people was elevated. However, we did not have a permanent location for our place of worship and training. I remember sitting on the stage at the hotel and beckoning to Edith. "Where are we going to continue meeting?" I asked.

"I don't know," she replied.

I told her to ask the hotel manger if we could continue our meeting at the hotel twice every month until we found a permanent location. To our surprise, the manager agreed.

After our Grand Opening, we began conducting training classes in my home. I was having a great time with the two new supporters who attended our very first classes. Edith and I would invite them to our home for dinner and good fellowship.

One of the ladies was our keyboardist and a singer; we would talk about the songs we could bring to enhance our worship experience. I encouraged her to play the keyboard for my sister's group. I felt she was a part of the Tabernacle of Praise family and that she was going to be a tremendous part of the organization; she seemed to be on board with the vision. However, the day before the last training classes, she called me to say she did not want to be part of the organization. She said God was leading her somewhere else.

I was devastated and hurt; she was the first person to leave and I took it personally. I considered this a serious wound, an injury that affected my heart and I did not understand why. At the time, I could not remember hearing anything from God. I prayed and asked God to give me courage and help me through. So I moved on and tried to keep my head up and embrace my new position as a leader. Along the way, God encouraged the ministry by sending family and friends to support our events, to visit, and to bless the organization financially. These acts of kindness kept me focused and inspired me to keep moving forward.

From Pain to Praise

> *The secret of success is learning how to use pain and pleasure instead of having pain and pleasure use you. If*

you do that, you're in control of your life. If you don't, life controls you.

-Anthony Robbins

Four months later we began planning a benefit dinner as a fund-raiser to further the organization. We were excited about the celebration. We sold tickets for the dinner and were preparing for a host of guests. Two weeks before our scheduled event, we went to the hotel for our regularly scheduled Sunday morning worship service. When we arrived, the doors of the hotel were locked. There was a sign on the door which said they filed bankruptcy and went out of business. WOW! What a blow to my heart! Here I am a young man with a family, in college trying to get my sociology degree and leading a non-profit organization to develop people's lives. I was only trying to obey God and yet another circumstance caused me pain.

I realized then that God is not moved by our circumstances. He is moved only by our faith and obedience. Once again, I did not know what to do. The benefit dinner was only weeks away and we had no location. I called my Bishop right away. At that time, Bishop W. W. Hamilton was my overseer. He told me not to worry and said we could have the service at Progressive Church of God in Christ during their Saturday meeting. Edith and I were so relieved and very grateful.

I asked my former pastor, James Davis, if we could use his church for a month at 12:00 noon for prayer and meditation, and he agreed. We had a great prayer meeting; our faith was strengthened and our hope was increased. At the end of the thirty days, God gave us a prophetic word through Pastor Davis. He said, "What God ordains He will sustain." These became words we have lived by throughout the duration of our ministry.

When the final prayer service was over, Edith and I went home. To our surprise, we were served with a subpoena to appear in court for custody of my stepdaughter. She was ten years old at that time. Edith and I had reared her together since she was four years old. I developed a great relationship with her; I even taught her to read.

The custody case was overwhelming, particularly because I did not have money for an attorney, and dealing with legal matters was all new to me. Of course, I was also a little nervous and afraid because I did not know what the outcome would be. We had three other children at that time and we did not want this situation to affect them. Also, we lived in Sacramento, but the subpoena was from a court in Fresno, three hours away. To top it off, Edith was seven months pregnant and already dealing with pre-term labor. The thought of traveling was unexpected and the entire situation broke our hearts. I thought to myself, "I only wanted to train and develop people; I didn't know I would face such challenges in my personal life."

> *No weapon that is formed against thee shall prosper;*
> *and every tongue that shall rise against thee in judgment*
> *thou shalt condemn. This is the heritage of the servants of the*
> *LORD, and their righteousness is of me, saith the LORD.*
> (Isaiah 54:17)

Edith and I immediately began to gather information from our daughter's school. Legally, the school district had to report any bruises on a child if they saw any. We also collected information from family, friends, and other community leaders that we felt proved we were fit parents and that the information in the court documents was not true. We were being accused of using electric cords to chastise our daughter on a regular basis. Edith heard the Lord say, "No weapon formed against you shall prosper. You will not need to fight in this battle. Stand still and see the salvation of the Lord."

When we arrived at the courthouse, we were assigned an attorney who fought for us and won the case without us showing the judge any of the information we had brought to defend ourselves. The whole ordeal made me question whether or not I wanted to keep doing this. I was wounded; nevertheless, I had to keep on going with my head up. During our benefit service I heard in my spirit that the experiences I was going to face would stretch, empower, and strengthen me to be the leader for the next generation. I did not know what it meant at the time, but as time went on I began to understand that my pain was designed to push me to praise God in spite of my circumstances.

The Challenge

If you want to achieve a high goal you're going to have to take some chances.

-Alberto Salazar

After the legal battle, we continued our search for a permanent location for the organization. The non-profit was three months old and did not really have enough finances to lease any of the buildings we found. Edith suggested that we have our worship services in our townhome until we could find a permanent location. I was thankful for her and her idea because at the time I was feeling the strain of dealing with my family, college and the church.

The next day, after I came home from college, Edith emptied out our living room and dining room and made them a place of worship. She put thirty chairs throughout the two rooms. We already had a keyboard in the house that played very nicely. We had already spoken with our neighbors; they were very nice and never complained about the sound. I invited my mother to be my first guest to speak and encourage the group to keep moving forward. On Sunday all thirty chairs were full, people received salvation and some were set free from addictions. Later, there were other speakers who also conducted revivals in my home. We never held back and we always gave God our best.

The Lord was blessing our services; however, since the keyboardist and singer left, I was playing the organ, singing and speaking. My former pastor, who was at that time my younger sister Rachel's pastor, allowed her to help with our praise and worship. My sister was nineteen years old at the time. She also attended Sacramento City College; we even had a speech class together. It was a blessing to have her working with me in the ministry.

Rachel was the youngest of nine siblings in my family. Growing up she was born with a heart condition, and the doctor told our mother that she would not live to be a little girl let alone a teenager, but she never allowed her condition to slow her down or stop her from assisting people, singing or being an encouragement to others. She was such a blessing to so many people that when the news came that she was engaged to be married, everyone that knew her was excited for her.

Keeping It Together

One Sunday after our 11:00 service, Edith, Rachel and I were invited to support my mother at a 3:00 service where she was speaking. Later that evening Rachel went with her fiancé to study for school. She was on the phone talking and laughing with my older sister Leisa when, without any warning at all, Leisa said, the phone dropped. Then she heard Rachel's fiancé yelling, "Oh my God! She passed out!"

He picked up the phone and asked Leisa, "What did you say to her? She is shaking!"

Leisa said, "Hang up the phone and call the paramedics."

On the way to the hospital, they confirmed that Rachel passed away while she was on the phone. Rachel died of a massive heart attack. I was distraught. What do I do? Do I stay in this place of hurt and defeat or do I keep going? I could not quit, so I continued to go on. The death of my sister was very difficult. The entire circumstance reminded me of my father, who had died exactly ten years earlier. This was more than an emotional wound; I felt this injury deep in my physical heart. I literally had to pray to keep my thoughts together.

*Thou wilt keep him in perfect peace, whose mind is
stayed on thee: because he trusteth in thee.* (Isaiah 26:3)

Two days after we buried my little sister Rachel, our newborn baby started crying as if she was in excruciating pain. We took Farrah (5 weeks old) to the hospital's emergency room, where they took x-rays of our baby's little body. The x-ray technician told us that Farrah had a reversed heart. When I asked him what that meant, he gave me a brief explanation and told me to talk to the doctor.

At that moment I thought to myself, "Should I just quit or should I curse God and die?" I could not believe this was happening to me just after burying my little sister, who had a similar condition. I did not want my daughter to suffer any pain. I saw what my parents went through with Rachel. Then I remembered how the Lord took care of my sister when the doctors wanted to perform surgery several times and my father said, "No." So I said, "If God can take care of Rachel, He can take care of Farrah too."

The doctor did a complete examination of Farrah and found out that she did not have a reversed heart after all. The technician had looked at the x-rays while Farrah was crying. When she cried, her body twisted and moved from side to side, which made her heart cross the middle line on the chart. We were so thankful the technician was wrong! The doctor prescribed an antibiotic and later, Farrah felt fine.

These are just some of the circumstances that wounded me right at the start of our new church. In each situation, I had to make a choice of moving forward or allowing my difficulties to control my destiny. I could have easily made excuses as to why I should quit or just give up. In fact, there was one preacher who said, "I'm glad you didn't quit when you moved the church into your home." I'd always thought that if a person said the Lord called him to the ministry, by faith he received the call for life. I knew in my spirit that quitting was not an option for me. There have been many leaders who have given up ministry because of difficulty. After the series of events I experienced when I accepted the call to ministry, I knew it was going to be a walk of faith.

That the trial of your faith, being much more precious than of gold that perishes, though it be tried with fire, might be found unto praise and honor and glory at the appearing of Jesus Christ: Whom having not seen, ye love; in whom, though now ye see him not, yet believing, ye rejoice with joy unspeakable and full of glory: Receiving the end of your faith, even the salvation of your souls. (1 Peter 1:7-9)

Home Base

Believe it or not, all of the events I just mentioned took place within six months after I started the organization. It was a lot of pressure for a twenty five year old pastor to experience. Nevertheless, I kept the faith and kept working with the help of God and the encouragement of my wife. The ministry continued in our home for another six months. I found myself in prayer three times a day asking God what to do and where to go. One day in prayer the Lord revealed Exodus 14:13 to me:

And Moses said unto the people, Fear ye not, standstill, and see the salvation of the LORD, which he will show to you today: for the Egyptians whom ye have seen today, ye shall see them again no more forever." (Exodus 14:13)

I said, "What do you mean stand still? I am praying and studying the Word of God, going through and holding on." Then God revealed to me that it meant, "Watch God work for you." At that moment, my faith was increased.

The leaders and supporters of the church were becoming restless in my home; we were in need of change. The majority of the supporters were receiving welfare or cash assistance. I could not depend on their financial support in leasing a new building. One day while I was praying, Edith received a call from one of the financially stable supporters. She said her boss, who was the director of the childcare center, wanted to know where we were meeting. When she told her we were meeting in my home, the director offered to let us use the *Children's World Daycare Center* for one year. When I spoke with the director, she said, "You don't need a credit check or any deposit; all you need to do is pay $400.00 per month."

We moved into the childcare center on February 6, 1996, one year after we started the organization. That was truly a blessing. We were paying the same amount when we were meeting at the hotel but were only allowed to have service one day a week, on Sunday. We were able to use the childcare center three days a week. I praised the Lord and had faith that we were back on the right track.

> *When life hands you a lemon, squeeze it and make lemonade.*
> -W. Clement Stone

During the time I went through these different difficulties, my mother told me, "If the enemy can destroy your family, he can destroy your church." She also said, "If you are not willing to fight the good fight of faith for your own wife and children, how much more will you fight for your businesses, ideas, health, others and the success of the organization?" I realized then that God was training me, increasing my faith and strengthening me to fight for what I believe. I learned it takes time to build a strong foundation in anything you do.

When I began the church, there were three other pastors who started churches at the same time. Within a couple of years, all three pastors closed their churches because they said they had no money. There were many times when I had no money, but by faith I always held onto the word that I heard, "Watch God work for you." I watched Almighty God work for me during these times, although I was creating other gods in my mind that I was not aware of.

Sparring Partner

One year after the church began, we were still excited. The ministry was moving forward and growing while we were meeting in the childcare center. We were witnessing, passing out flyers, meeting people and inviting them to church. We were in a campaign for souls and we wanted God to add to the church daily.

The spring semester began at Sacramento City College. I remember thinking, "I need more support at the church." I wanted God to bless me with the right person to assist me in the early stages of our ministry.

> *The ascent of Everest was not the work of one day, nor*
> *even of those few unforgettable weeks in which we climbed*
> *… it is in fact a tale of sustained and tenacious endeavors by*
> *many, over a long period of time.*
>
> -Sir John Hunt

During my spring semester at Sacramento City College, I took a class called African-American History. There were a few African American men enrolled, including my professor, who was a very candid, intimidating, no-nonsense instructor. One of the students in the class looked like one of my brothers-in-law. We never spoke in class; we just gave each other the classic head nod. One day I was sitting in class, and in my spirit I heard, "He is your assistant. He will work close to you and he will serve in the ministry." I said to myself, "Yeah right!"

After class I introduced myself to him and told him that I went to church and that I was a pastor. He said his name was Eric Barnes and he had just moved to Sacramento from Los Angeles. He said he was a Christian, too, and was looking for a church home. We continued to talk for a good while and had a rather enjoyable conversation. He came to a worship service one Sunday and joined the church. I could not believe it. The words God spoke to me came to pass quickly.

We labored in the childcare center for one year. By the time the lease was up, the membership had increased and we out grew the space. However, our revenue did not increase. I wish I had known then what I know now.

Chapter 1   Wrestling Lessons

You will notice there are wrestling lessons throughout this book which are designed to make you think about the oppositions and obstacles in your life and help you observe and evaluate your mental standpoint.

1. How do you generally react when unforeseen circumstances happen?

_____

_____

_____

_____

_____

2. How often do you allow your negative circumstances to hinder you from moving forward?

_____

_____

_____

_____

_____

3. Name some circumstances that wounded you and from which you have not yet healed.

_____

_____

_____

_____

Chapter 1   Wrestling Strategies

Wrestling strategies are used as instructions for what to do in difficult situations. When you find yourself in complicated circumstances, refer back to these as useful tips to apply to your circumstance in everyday life.

1. When faced with a crisis, before jumping to conclusions:
    *   Investigate the problem thoroughly.
    *   Get wisdom and understanding before you move forward.
    *   Never do or say anything that you will regret or cannot fix.
    *   If you cannot fix it, pray about it and move on.

2. When dealing with negative issues:
    *   Find something positive in the situation.
    *   If you are not familiar with what you are dealing with, seek out the right mentor or information.
    *   Always acknowledge God and He will direct you.

3. If you find that you are wounded from past situations:
    *   Forgive those who have hurt you.
    *   Release it before it becomes bitterness and resentment.
    *   Time will heal, if you keep your faith in God's Word.

CHAPTER 2

CHALLENGES
EMBRACING VICTORY

Our lives improve only when we take chances and the
first and most difficult risk we can take is to be honest with
ourselves.

-Walter Anderson

I heard the Victory Outreach Church had moved and that their building was for lease or sale. The building had been converted from a movie theatre into a church. Edith and I took a look at the building and fell in love with it. I remembered saying to myself, "This will be a great opportunity to work at this level and I am excited about what we are going to embark upon." I asked the pastor of Victory Outreach if I could have a meeting with our church members in the building.

The following week we scheduled a meeting and took the members to see the building. When the meeting was over, the members were very excited. After we met, I scheduled a meeting with the pastor and he agreed to enter into a lease/purchase agreement. The pastor came up with the terms, which were a little out of reach for my thirty-member church, but I was young and full of faith. I did not worry about the money because I believed that God would make a way.

The Victory Outreach Church had a men's home that ran a very successful carwash. They averaged at least $2000.00 a month. I thought that if we leased the property, we could continue the carwash and have that flow of income. After the negotiations, I explained to the members of our church the amount of the lease and the terms. I also explained that the carwash could make up the difference of what we needed. We really were depending on the carwash.

In the meantime we mailed letters to family members and friends, requesting support for what we needed to move in, but received no response. The pastor even allowed us to have our church anniversary in the building in order to raise the money we needed. The anniversary was a success. We had a host of speakers and friends who came to support our efforts.

On the last night, a long time family friend Reverend Glen Taylor from Reno, Nevada was our guest speaker. After he preached he said he wanted to be a blessing to the ministry and gave us a donation of $3,000.00. My wife began to cry because that was what we needed to secure the agreement for the building.

The members seemed excited and I was thankful to the Lord for the opportunity. However, to my great surprise, when it was time to move into the building, most of the members left the church. I was crushed and shocked. I could not believe it; the same people who seemed so excited and proud to be members left the church. Most of them left because they were dealing with their own problems and situations. Others, however, left because they did not want to commit to the church at another level. In the end, there were only five members left and half of them were on welfare. I prayed and cried, thinking, "What did I get myself into?"

Rookies and Professionals

We keep going back, stronger, not weaker, because we will not allow rejection to beat us down. It will only strengthen our resolve, to be successful there is no other way.
-Earl G. Graves

There I was, in a church that seated 200 people, with only five members. We had already signed the contract and were in the building; it was sink or swim. We had to focus on rebuilding with five people. Again, I had to pray, speak, play the organ and sing for the praise and worship service. I had faith that God would see us through.

My assistant, Minister Barnes, was the only one I could count on to work the carwash with me. Those were very difficult days at times. One day it was so challenging that Minister Barnes was ready to move back to Los Angeles; but he did not. He had so much faith that God would bless the ministry that he was willing to make major sacrifices. He quit his job to help me wash cars. His commitment to the ministry encouraged me and gave me strength on many occasions down through the years and still does to this day.

> *Success is the sum of small efforts, repeated day in and day out.*
>
> -Robert Collier

As time went on, the carwash was not bringing in the revenue we thought it would. Most of the clients of the carwash were patrons of the Wells Fargo Bank that was next door to the church. People would park their cars at the church for a carwash while they went into the bank. Right after we took over the carwash, the bank relocated and there was less traffic in the area. This resulted in a very slow carwash business and less money than anticipated.

My wife was also very dedicated to the ministry. Edith has always been willing to do whatever was needed to ensure that the work of the Lord progressed. By this time we had six children. Our latest son was only seven weeks old. Edith and I were preparing to move. We were already approved and were excited about making a change in our home.

When the time came to make the church's lease payment, there was not enough money in the church's account. So Edith and I decided to ask my mother that if we gave our money to the church, could our family stay at her house for a month or two. She said yes. We gave all of our money to the church, including the rent and deposit for our new home, to ensure that the lease was paid.

This was a very difficult time for Edith. Ever since leaving her mother's house she had always lived on her own. When I met Edith she was twenty-one years old with an apartment that was fully furnished with brand new furniture. She has always taken pride in her home and the contents therein. First, she welcomed the church into her home, and then she gave up her home to pay the church's lease payment. What an extraordinary woman! She was more than committed to the ministry; she was embracing our future with faith and expectancy.

I was going to the church every morning at 6 o'clock, praying for direction and spiritual power. I believed that God would add to the church and send in the revenue needed to sustain us. Now that I look back, I believe that God has given every ministry a means to bring in additional income outside of tithes and offering. Victory Outreach made an impact with the carwash because they already had established clients. They were able to supplement their income for the church. Our church did not do as well because the bank closed and took the clients.

In my early ministry, I learned that a pastor must know their church's own strengths and weaknesses. This revelation does not come from watching other ministries or copying their format. This comes from much prayer, fasting and time.

Even though the church was not raising enough money to pay all of the bills on time, I kept my head up, kept praying and thanked the Lord for favor. It was certainly a journey, because I was trying with all my heart to please God by doing Kingdom work. The enemy was really trying to attack me to make me throw in the towel.

I remember going to my mother's house one day after washing cars from sunup until sundown. Out of the blue, one of my sisters began to go off on me. She said in a loud tone, "You need to tell God to give you a raise!"

Hang in There

It's always too soon to quit. -Norman Vincent Peale

I was hurt to the core of my heart because I felt like I was doing all I knew how to do. I was already dealing with the responsibilities of the church and its finances, not counting the fact that I was fulltime in ministry. I gave all my money to the church in order for it to succeed. However, I was still wondering if God was going to bless me and the church. I went to my room and fell on my face. I began to pray with tears streaming down my face. I was broken about many things. I told God how I was feeling and how bewildered I was about the entire ministry situation. After I gave God my heartfelt speech, God spoke to me and gave me a scripture:

> But the wisdom that is from above is first pure, then peaceable, gentle, and easy to be entreated, full of mercy and good fruits, without partiality, and without hypocrisy. (James 3:17)

Keep Your Eyes on the Prize

> It's easy to be negative and unmotivated, but it takes some work to be positive and motivated. While there's no off button for those relentless tapes, there are things that you can do to turn down the volume and shift your focus from the negative to the positive.
>
> -Donna Cardillo

God let me know He was still with me. I learned something very valuable during this experience; you never let what someone says stop you from focusing on what God gave you to do. When God speaks a word, it uplifts and corrects you with love and purity, not with hypocrisy. I cheered up and moved on. We continued to pray and believed God for a miracle.

The church was not growing as fast as we had hoped. However, my spiritual man was being shaped drastically. Since the carwash failed to bring in finances, Minister Barnes and I began going into the community witnessing and passing out flyers. We walked for miles witnessing and trying to build the church. One day after witnessing, I came back to the church and the Holy Spirit began to question me about our flyers.

He asked me, "What do you think of your flyer?"

"I think it looks nice," I said.

"Would you come to your church if you received this flyer?" He asked.

I looked at the flyer for a few moments and then said, "No, because it does not say what the church teaches or believes in."

The flyer was a black and white, 8 ½ by 11 photo copy that read, "Join us every Sunday morning at 11am for our morning worship services."

Then the Holy Spirit said, "I want you to go on television."

Since we had very little membership growth and no money or equipment to do a television program, it seemed impossible. That's when I realized that if I wasn't willing to obey the Holy Spirit even when I didn't understand, how could I expect Him to trust me to do His will?

At the word of the Holy Spirit I began to research information on how to begin a television program. I called R.C.C.T.V., (which is a local cable television station) and the program director answered the phone. Her name was Jeanie. She scheduled an appointment with me to discuss the possibility of a television program. I was so excited and yet frightened at the fact that I had no idea what to expect or how to even format a program. So I did what I always did when I found myself between a rock and a hard place in my ministry: I prayed. As I prayed, the Holy Spirit began to speak and told me to call the telecast *"Set Free."*

I was so excited! I told those who were in prayer with me what the Holy Spirit had said. To this day, sixteen years later, the name remains the same for all of my radio and television productions.

For as the body without the spirit is dead, so faith without works is dead also. (James 2:26)

I went to the meeting with the program director, realizing that I had no way of producing my own show. She asked me questions about the type of broadcast I had in mind. I shared with her my vision of a television program and what the focus would be. After I explained the concept, I also told her that I did not have any production equipment.

She said, "Oh, that's fine. We are beginning our own in-house production and if you'd like, you can be our very first television production."

I was so thrilled. I knew I had heard the voice of God. The Lord knew that I did not have the equipment, but He knew that R.C.C.T.V. did. All I had was my faith. When Jeanie asked, "What is the name of your program?" I really did not want to tell her, thinking she would be critical of the name. Then, out of the blue, she said, "Why don't you call your show, *Set Free?*"

I could not believe it. I told her, "That is the same name the Holy Spirit gave me!" My *Set Free* television ministry began with the favor of God. I was energized about this opportunity to be on television. I had never imagined being on television and I realized that it wasn't me; it was God who wanted it to be so.

Another Round

Two months after we moved into the building, we were still hoping that washing cars would pick up financially. One day as we were working, a Hispanic man came to the church needing a place to live. I prayed about it, and in exchange for his support washing cars and cleaning the church, I allowed him to stay in the church.

After a while, there began to be conflict between the Hispanic man and Minister Barnes. I laid down a few rules and told the man I would not tolerate any disrespect, and if he was going to continue to stay there, he had to abide by the rules. I also told him that I would never put him out on the streets. If it came down to it, I would take him to a shelter or somewhere else safe. When the time came, that is exactly what I did; I took him to the Victory Outreach men's home.

The assistant to the pastor of Victory Outreach was a young man who visited our church from time to time, encouraging us. He would tell us stories of what God had done through his life. I did not mind; I tried to be kind to everyone.

One day during our third month in the building, the young man came to the church and told me that he was no longer with the ministry because of things he was tired of seeing. I tried to encourage him to stay at Victory Outreach and pray about it. I did not want to be caught in the middle between him and his pastor because he came to me as a brother in Christ.

Two weeks later, as Minister Barnes and I were outside washing cars, the young man stopped by again to see how we were doing. Immediately after he arrived, the pastor of his church drove up. The young man started to leave, but I told him not to; after all, we were just talking.

Blind Sided

Obstacles are what you see when you take your eyes off the goal.

-Unknown

The pastor got out of his car and went off on me. He told me that he was coming back to this building to do the carwash and that we would not be able to use the area for washing cars anymore. He came back a little later and said, "I was going to assist you in purchasing the building, but because you befriended my enemy, the deal is off! Furthermore, you have one week to get out of my building!"

Just like that. With no warning notice or any further explanation, he was kicking us out. I felt totally confused because I never saw this coming. Once again I was in the position of not knowing where we were going to have services.

What was I going to do? I prayed about it and asked God what to do. That is when I began to understand that in ministry you will go through many challenging and difficult situations. However, you can make it and continue to move forward in the strength of the Lord. It's tough at times, but you must fight the good fight of faith and continue on the journey if you want to experience victory. This unexpected turn of events opened the door for a god of doubt and worry to begin to develop in my subconscious mind.

On the Road Again

Learn to get in touch with the silence within yourself and know that everything in life has a purpose.
-Elisabeth Kubler-Ross MD

As we were packing and moving boxes into the truck to take to storage, I begin to reflect on the last two years of our journey. I wondered what in the world we should do now! I began to think about the fluctuation of membership from zero to thirty and then thirty to five; hotel problems; the townhouse; the childcare center; and now this, another move. In my subconscious I was erecting another god of uncertainty. I remember saying, "I hope that after this, the members we have will stick by us."

We were finished loading the truck and I was ready to go. Edith was still inside the church cleaning and making sure we did not leave anything behind. I kept trying to rush her because I just wanted to get away from that place. I cannot adequately describe how frustrated I felt, moving after only three months in the building. I was ready to settle the ministry and have church.

As we loaded the truck, a friend of the family who I hadn't seen for many years stopped by. He asked me how things were going, and I shared with him what had happened with the pastor of the church and why we were moving. He gave me his number and told me to let me know if I needed any help with my next move. I praised God for the timing and for allowing me to come into contact with him just before we drove off. Ironically, I also thanked the Lord for Edith taking her time. Had we left any sooner, I would have never connected with an old friend who was instrumental in donating the resources to get into our next facility.

Chapter 2   Wrestling Lessons

In chapter two we learned that just because you go through challenges does not mean you cannot experience victories. Here are some lessons to think about.

1. Take time to identify the major challenges in your life and then list several practical steps you can take to address those challenges.

_____

_____

_____

_____

2. List some practical ways that you can embrace and capitalize on victories that you win.

_____

_____

_____

_____

3. List some empowering words to help you keep your focus in the midst of challenges.

_____

_____

_____

_____

4. Lists several pieces of inspirational music that speak particularly to your heart.

_____

_____

_____

_____

Chapter 2   Wrestling Strategies

Here are some strategies that helped me when I was faced with difficult challenges.

1. How do you handle your challenges?
    *   Think positive thoughts; I can do all things through Christ.
    *   Embrace good thoughts; my belief in myself is changing my circumstances.
    *   Constantly remind yourself that nothing can stop you with out your permission.

2. How do you bring change to your challenges?
    *   Change your way of thinking.
    *   Surround yourself with positive people.
    *   Don't let challenges overwhelm you.
    *   Remember that every day is a new day.

3. Write down decisions that will move you forward.

    _____

    _____

    _____

    _____

    _____

4. Write down your most challenging goals.

    _____

    _____

    _____

    _____

    _____

WRESTLING FOR POSSESSION

The indispensable first step to getting the things you want out of life is this; decide what you want.

- Ben Stein

The crippled man who waited at the pool of Bethesda for thirty-eight years (see John 5:1-9) reminds me of the children of Israel who wandered for forty years in the wilderness (see Num. 14:26-35). In both stories an opportunity to be blessed in the early stages of the journey of life is forfeited due to circumstances and/or decisions made on a daily basis. The crippled man in Jerusalem and rebellious children of Israel in the wilderness both exhibit lack of faith and a failure to realize that the hardship they endure is actually a test designed to prepare them for their blessings, not cripple or hinder them.

The man who lay at the pool became comfortable in his crippled condition. While waiting all those long years for healing, he became a beggar and a burden to his friends and others around him. How many times do we inconvenience people because of the choices we make? The crippled man lay there by the side of the pool waiting for someone else to help him, when what he needed to do was support himself.

You cannot wait forever for someone to give you support. I did not understand this until we moved the ministry to a new location and the people I expected to assist us never came. I had a choice: to lie at the pool or to embrace my future in the Lord.

Never let anyone talk you out of your visions and dreams that God has given you.

- John Wynn

My ministerial journey in Sacramento was very demanding. In my view of the journey, it was a wilderness experience. I saw God sustain the ministry against great odds. When God gives you an assignment, He gives you the knowledge, resources, and time necessary to carry it out. Sometimes, as a leader, you find that your parishioners do not always understand the road you have taken. Many times they try to redirect the vision. You learn that you cannot allow people to distract your focus. If I had let people persuade me to change my focus with their money or negative comments, we would have wandered much longer than we did.

After we finished moving out of Victory Outreach Church, I was discouraged, tired, my body was hurting and I had become very sick with the flu. Before I went home I wanted to talk to someone. I knew the search was on for a new place to worship, and I needed a moment to vent. However, I also needed to hear the voice of someone with faith and understanding.

I went to see Bishop George Archie because I knew he was a man of prayer and faith. I opened up to Bishop Archie about the trials I had been going through and explained the conflict with Pastor Jones (not his real name) and how our building was ripped right out from under us! He sat quietly and listened as I poured my heart out. When you have been through spiritual battles, it is important to talk to people of faith who are not judgmental and will not discourage you or make you think negatively about your circumstances.

The number one problem that keeps people from winning in the United States today is lack of belief in themselves.
-Arthur L. Williams

If you connect to the wrong source when you are going through a test or trial, it can cripple you. God wants a testimony out of you, not a death sentence. Bishop Archie shared his testimonies with me; many were experiences of his building process of their new church. After our conversation, I was encouraged and ready to continue my journey. Before I left, Bishop Archie offered us the use of his former church building, which sat directly behind the new one, for our worship services.

This was a great and unexpected opportunity. I began rejoicing and praising the Lord. I said, "God does not open a new door until the old one closes." I thought again about the pastors who had started at the same time I did, but quit. I could not help but wonder whether, if they had held on by faith, the Lord would have continued to work things out for them. When you work for Christ and you have heard and accepted the call, you must be focused on kingdom work, not money. You do it because you trust God and believe He is the one who called you.

When I arrived home, I immediately went to bed and fell asleep. A short time later, Edith came home. She had been driving around all day praying and asking God to reveal another location. She walked into the bedroom and said, "John you have to come see this. I think I found our new church building." I asked where it was, but she would not tell me.

Without delay, I was dressed and in the car. She drove me to Sky Parkway and 65th Street. I thought she was taking me to the old Oshman's Sports 10,000 square foot building that we looked at two years before, but I was wrong. She passed the entrance to that building and then stopped in front of the next one. Right next door to the old Oshman's building was another empty building, formerly a Fabric Land store. This building was 8,000 square feet.

Looking on in amazement I said, "I can't believe this vacant building is right next door to the one we looked at two years ago!" I immediately called Minister Barnes and asked him to meet us. He came right over. All of us stood outside that building looking through the windows in complete astonishment.

So many different emotions swirled through my mind as I stood there. I felt outraged but could not pinpoint the object of my anger. Was I angry at the pastor who had put my congregation out on the street or was I angry at myself for signing a contract with him in the first place?

After pondering and rehashing all the trials of building a church from scratch, I decided I was angry at satan for always frustrating my plans and purpose. Or was I indeed angry at God?

All I know is that I stood outside that building with a million things going through my mind. My body was fatigued and I was very sore. On top of that, I had a fever. All of a sudden, I saw in my mind the building set up like a church. I saw the pulpit and the pews. I knew exactly how I could organize everything, including the offices. I thought, "Surely, this is my fever causing me to think this way." The next thing I knew I asked Minister Barnes, "Do you think we can do this?"

He replied, "With God, we can do anything."

The longer I stood there, the more my faith increased and I began to encourage myself in the Lord.

> And David was greatly distressed; for the people spoke of stoning him, because the soul of all the people was grieved, every man for his sons and for his daughters: but David encouraged himself in the LORD his God. (1 Samuel 30:6)

Believing in Yourself is an Attitude

> You weren't an accident. You weren't mass produced. You aren't an assembly-line product. You were deliberately planned, specifically gifted, and lovingly positioned on the Earth by the Master Craftsman.
>
> -Max Lucado

> I can do all things through Christ which strengthens me. (Philippians 4:13)

It is important that leaders surround themselves with men and women who believe in their vision. I prayed about this location and then called my cousin, who knew real estate like the back of his hand. Since the building was in disrepair and needed carpet, paint and other cosmetic repairs, we wrote an offer that required $10,000.00 in tenant improvements. We also requested two months free rent and that the rent be lowered. The total move-in required $5,000.00, which I did not have. In any case, the owner of the building accepted all our terms and conditions. The previous weekend, our family had moved out of my mother's house and into our own place. Our children were glad to be in a home of their own again. God was restoring all that we had lost.

As we were unpacking and getting settled, the real estate agent called and said that the contract for the building was ready for me to sign. I said I would come the next day, which was Friday. Normally, when you sign a contract they expect the money to accompany it; however, I didn't have any money, having just relocated my family and bought groceries. For a 27 year-old man with a wife and six children, I felt blessed and was praising the Lord just to have accomplished that. I did not have an extra $5,000.00 just lying around. When I operate in faith, there's a feeling of gratitude and thanksgiving that comes over me and I can see beyond limits. When I sense this, I release all fear, doubt and worry...and good things happen.

When we arrived to sign the contract, I told the agent that I would have a cashier's check for $5,000.00 on Monday morning. After I said that, I don't really know what happened; all I know is that I felt good! A smile came over my face. I have always believed it was my faith being activated.

After leaving the real estate office, Edith and I began discussing this ambitious venture we were embarking upon. As soon as I arrived home, I called the family friend who had told me to call him if I needed help with my next move. We talked for a while and I brought him up to speed with our situation. I told him that I needed $5000.00 in a cashier's check by Monday morning in order to secure the deal

He said, "Okay, let me check some things out and I will get back with you."

I was not worried at all. Nor was I nervous, because my faith was working. I felt it working; I don't ever remember feeling so calm. When I look back on it now, the thought that comes to mind is, "I MUST

HAVE BEEN CRAZY!" Either my faith was activated; I was completely out of my mind, or both! The weekend came and went with no phone call from my friend. I believed that God was going to touch his heart and make a way. "After all," I thought, "why wouldn't God make a way for someone to be a blessing to His church?"

By noon I couldn't wait any longer, so I called him. He said, "Meet me at your mother's house." When my friend arrived, he said, "I'm going to loan you this $5,000, however, I want you to pay me back."

"Okay," I said, but I felt a little disappointed. I thought he was going to bless the church with a donation; I hadn't expected it to be a loan. But when he put that check in my hand, I took a deep breath, and at that moment I literally felt the manifestation of faith. A deep sense of assurance filled me and rested in my spirit.

We moved into the building in June, 1997. Minister Barnes and I worked endless hours to ensure that the building looked like a church. We wanted the people of God to walk in the door ready to praise the Lord without any distractions. I desired to build a platform 36ft long and 3ft high. I knew it was going to be extremely expensive. Edith called around to many different wood supply companies to see if we could get plywood donated. She finally found a company that agreed to give us the majority of what we needed.

After we had the supplies, we needed the manpower to take on this project. I called a member of my stepfather's church to ask him if he would help me. He said he could get me started, but we needed someone with more experience to make sure we were doing it right. He called a retired contractor who was also a member of my step-father's church. The team came together and began to work diligently. Our goal was to complete the platform by the end of the week, before the carpet was to be installed. We worked day and night. The Lord sent different men from other churches to assist us, which was a great blessing.

By the end of the week we were finished with the platform and ready for the carpet. However, the painting was not finished. The painter painted the walls but never came back to paint the ceiling. The ceiling was off-white and the walls were light blue. At this point there was nothing we could do. Before we knew it, the installers had shown up and were laying the carpet. "Oh well," I said to Edith, "we tried. We will just have a dirty look on the ceiling."

Due to the size of the building, it would have been very difficult to spray-paint the ceiling and protect $8,000.00 of brand new carpet. What else could I do? I will never forget the look on our faces as we stood there when the men rolled out 6,000 square feet of blue carpet and the entire ceiling turned blue. We were amazed! It suddenly looked like we *had* painted the ceiling.

We were so grateful finally to have a place of worship, and we immediately began preparing for our first service. We rented chairs, invited people and even engaged a guest speaker. By the night of the first service, I was sick again. I had been working industriously without resting or eating, and my body finally said, "Stop!"

But of course, I did not. Looking back, I wish I had; maybe then I wouldn't have endured so much. I could not make it to church, so I stayed in bed and worshiped the Lord for the marvelous things He had done. My faith never wavered; it was at a new level. I believed God would do what He said He would do.

God will give you what you ask for. However, it is important to take time to see the whole picture before you pray and make your request known to the Lord. I learned that when you walk in faith, you still have to count the cost. I have always been a man of vision and faith. What I did not know was that my faith at this new level would be severely tested for the next two years.

As we continued on television, our ministry grew. There were families joining the church, as well as young single men and women. As the growth came, we remained steadfast in prayer and fasting. We had a noon prayer service Monday through Friday; people came on their lunch break and brought their friends. The Lord was truly blessing the people and they were glad. The excitement increased when people began receiving salvation, deliverance and the gift of the Holy Spirit. It was awesome watching God bless the church. I looked forward to going to the church every day for prayer because that was where I found my strength.

God used me in the gift of prophecy, but I felt like I needed some direction in the work of the ministry. I was at a point in my life when I knew my gift needed to be sharpened. I developed a strong personal relationship and communication with God, but felt I needed much more. I began reading different books, searching for information that could take me to another level. I did not really know how I was going to get there; I just knew I needed a shift in my life.

One day I attended a church conference with my brother-in-law where a prophet spoke very profoundly. My brother-in-law purchased some of his videos and let me borrow them when I went home. I was blessed by his teaching on prayer. Since I was going through such a transitional point in my life, I thought this was exactly what I had been searching for: sound prophetic teaching to catapult me to my next dimension.

I called the number on the screen and asked the prophet if he would be my guest for a revival in Sacramento, California.

"I would love to come," he said.

This man had a very unique ministry, one that portrayed excellence at a powerful level. He seemed to be one who diligently sought the face of God and had experienced an enormous amount of encounters in the spirit realm. I was right. I knew exactly what I needed; someone to coach me who had experience in the prophetic. I also knew he would take the church to another level, and I was right about that as well. When you are sincerely trying to seek the face of God in areas where you may not have previously experienced Him, He will send people into your life to aide and equip you for your assignment.

After the prophet accepted my invitation, I immediately began airing his video tapes on my telecast for an entire month, advertising that he would be in revival with us. When he arrived in the city, our services were packed with spectators every night for an entire week. It was a powerful revival. For the very first time I had the experience of being around a man who poured ministry into me during the church service as well as outside of church. He gave me so much information, revelation, knowledge and instruction that my head would be tired when I arrived home at the end of the night. He even gave Edith and me information regarding our health.

At the end of the revival, we were walking along together when the prophet said, "You will pastor more than one church."

I said, "Yeah, right," and kept walking.

I do not know if my response was because of all the frustration I was experiencing as a young man in ministry with only one church. I may have responded in that manner because no one showed me how to operate the church at its inception, which is what caused my frustration in the first place. I prayed for miracles and asked God to bring change to our circumstances, but the more I prayed, the more challenging things became. Surely I did not want to deal with that in more than one church!

Most of the financial problems I dealt with, such as the rent, the power bill, and the insurance, did not need a miracle; I just needed to raise the money. I remember one time when we could not pay $2,500.00 for the church's electric bill and it was turned off over the weekend. It was a very large building with an extreme amount of lighting. The blessing was that the entire front wall of the building was all glass. It was fine because we had good light during the day so we were still able to have Sunday morning service. We rented a generator for the sound equipment and had a great time in the Lord. God blessed us and after the service we raised enough money to turn the lights back on Monday morning.

It is said that in times past, if a young man felt the leading to pastor a church, the older pastors gave no advice; they just said, "God bless you." Today's society has changed. I have noticed there are more self-help books than ever before. When you go to the bookstore you can find books with the entire blueprint of a ministry from start to finish. Unfortunately, I had no book, no blueprint and no man to guide me through the ups and downs of a young ministry. I had to be processed in a way in which God could get all of the glory out of my life. God did not want me or anyone else to take credit for what He was going to do in my life. However, every now and then the Lord would allow someone to cross my path with a prophetic word or a nugget of wisdom that I would hold onto dearly. You can image how much these words of encouragement meant to me. When someone began to pour out wisdom and knowledge, I soaked them up like a sponge.

After the prophet left the city, I went on a six-day fast. I believed God for miracles as well as for more growth of the church. One day as I was praying and walking around the church, I heard God say, "You are nothing but a vessel." At that moment, I realized that since I was going to be used for His glory, I would not have control of my ministry. I also realized that I was being developed for ministry and that I was on a journey to discover who John Wynn was.

This time of my life was incredible because I was trying to keep a roof over my own head as well as the church's head, bring in income for my family and income for the church. I felt as if I had to work double time to make dual things happen for my family as well as for the church. At the time, I was an Adult Education Substitute Teacher for the Grant Unified School District. I was not receiving a salary from the church.

One day I went to the church to pray and ended up praying all night by myself. As I prayed, I heard the Lord speak to me and say, "I want you to stop working and go back to fulltime ministry." That same night the Lord said, "You will never work on a secular job in the city of Sacramento again." Even though the Lord told me I would not work again; there were times when I needed to make provision for my family, so I still looked for a job. There were many days I actually cried because I did everything to get a job or find work of some kind, but I was unsuccessful.

The Lord always encouraged me by leading someone to call me to speak at a church or a conference. He would open doors for me to minister and it would literally blow my mind to see the reception of the Word. People would be blessed and I would be encouraged so that I would forget about not having a job. I would make more money ministering than I had working for the school district, the Internal Revenue Service, First Interstate Bank or any of my other previous jobs. This season was part of my wilderness experience when I had to trust God no matter what.

The church began to grow and the finances began to increase, but we were four months behind in the rent. It felt like a losing battle with the landlord. I prayed every day and witnessed the move of God, but we still could not catch up with the church's rent. Because I really did not know how to operate the church with the minimal finances we were bringing in, things got worse. I was at the point of wanting to share our needs with the members, not realizing that it was too late. I did not know how to share it with members who were not members when we began to fall behind in our payments.

We went through this battle because I was not focused on God as much as I thought I was, and not nearly as much as I needed to be. I was too consumed with trying to keep the building. One night we prayed so hard for the landlord and called his name out that my sister thought we were praying for a church member who was in the hospital.

I did not realize that the building had become the center of my attention. My thoughts were consumed with ideas such as; "If we witness, we can gain more members to support us; then we will not lose the building." And, "We need to pray that the people give their tithes and offering so we won't lose the building." I let my focus shift to the building and away from the vision and mission that God had given me. So another false god took up residence in my consciousness: the god of distractions.

I remember one powerful service where the preaching was effective, souls were saved and set free from sin, and impartation took place from the laying on of hands from me and my team of intercessors. It was awesome to see the move of God in the service. However, when it was time for the ministry of giving, we raised $400. It was very frustrating because the budget was $4,000, and the budget for the month needed to be met during the general offering. We needed the $4,000 to pay the monthly lease that day, and I was surprised that we didn't meet the budget after such a powerful service. I know it is not that God doesn't care about us, the church or the vision; however, He teaches us that He is our source, not man. This was one of the worst experiences of ministry up to that point, but it was a pivotal point that changed my entire perspective.

I believe that through that experience I actually had an encounter with God that pushed me to another level in ministry. For one thing, my preaching was stronger. I studied God's Word and prayed. On three different occasions I fasted six days and nights. Several times, I stayed in the church all night. My heart was right and I continued to seek more of God's presence. However, my focus was still wrong. I was trying to increase my spiritual man, thinking it was going to change my financial difficulties. I realized that just because I sought the face of God did not mean He was going to automatically bring me out of my financial problems.

I was a young leader trying to keep all the financial challenges between myself and the board, not giving any information to the members of the church. When I attended school, they taught me the mechanics of preaching and how to study the Word of God, but not how to handle pastoral issues that are unique to a particular congregation. Neither did they teach me how to pastor a church with a faith budget. I felt helpless, because I did not go to school to learn how to be a pastor, prophet, teacher and business man; there were no classes to educate me on faith. I had to learn through my experiences. I realized that in order to understand that God is our source and He has a plan for us, we must go through wilderness experiences. A wilderness experience exposes your heart focus and your faith.

> *Every negative event contains within it the seed of an equal or greater benefit.*
> - Napoleon Hill

After struggling with the rent for two years, and praying, fasting and preaching about faith, we still did not have the finances we needed to maintain our facility. But we never stopped ministry. We continued to do the work of the Lord. The church was finally growing. We put the vision on the wall and even had a building fund campaign called "Operation Possession." Our cable television ministry was a blessing to many people. We were excited about what was going on. In fact, we had just launched our school, called "Top Academy," for K through 12th grade. We put two portable buildings in the back of the facility to accommodate the classrooms.

I had crazy faith but I never counted the cost. Consequently, even after preaching on faith and that God would make a way out of no way, our church still had to move out of that building. I was in a very uncomfortable position because I didn't know how to tell the members. Confused and emotional, I asked God over and over, "Why? Why didn't you give us the money to maintain the building? Why at this point in ministry?" I could not understand why God would allow me to come to such a place in the ministry and not fulfill what I felt He told me to do. I waited for an answer, but God was not ready to give me one yet.

> *Wait on the LORD: be of good courage, and he shall strengthen thine heart: wait, I say, on the LORD.* (Psalm 27:14)

The following Sunday, I preached on the topic, "Get Your Stuff, and Let's Go." I took my text from the Book of Numbers, when the children of Israel had to leave Egypt to go and possess the land that God had promised to them. I let the congregation know that the building was not our promised land and that we must move forward to obtain what God had for us.

We came back that night and moved out of the building. I was devastated! The people did not know what to expect, yet they believed in me and followed me as I tried to follow Christ. The board knew what was going on, but we did not let the other members know until it was too late. The work we put into the building, the labor for growth of the church, the prayer and shut-in ministries we did for the power of God to be with us; and now we had come to this?

Our plan had been to own the current building and the movie theater directly behind it. Suddenly, all our grand plans and desires had vanished like smoke. At this point in my life my thought process was, "Sink or swim, have faith or quit, walk away or continue." It was amazing to see how our church had grown and how our vision was coming to pass. I never dreamed that God would allow us to lose that building.

To make things worse, I was now being criticized by outsiders and former members. I was like the crippled man lying at the pool of Bethesda. My faith had just been crippled. I had to find a new location in order to continue the ministry. Once again, I asked myself and the board, "Should we stop, or should we keep on going? What should we do?" Obviously, this was a very difficult time for me in ministry and I thought that it could not possibly get any worse. But when the rumors started circulating and people in the community began questioning me, I realized it *was* worse. I decided I had to pray very hard just to continue to fight. The hurt inside was so bad that I fasted three days and nights.

> *Never give up on your dreams...Perseverance is all important. If you didn't have the desire and the belief in yourself to keep trying after you've been told you should quit, you'll never make it.*
>
> - Tawni O' Dell

I truly thank the Lord every day for my wife, who continues to stay by my side. She loves God, loves the ministry, and always encourages me to keep on going. I learned through the difficulties I experienced that it is important that a man marries a wife who is compatible with him for the ministry. A man's wife can make or break their ministry. If he's not praying and asking God to bless him with the wife who is assigned to him, it could be a catastrophe. Many times the enemy attacks a leader or a pastor through his mate in order to bring distraction and destruction to the entire ministry. A praying wife who knows how to cover the ministry with love and prayer is precious and priceless.

It was because Edith remained faithful in prayer that I was able to stay focused. Whenever I felt like I was losing hope or getting off course because of losing the building, she reminded me of what the Word of God said. One night I found myself praying in faith and believing instead of being frustrated, and then God gave me an answer. It wasn't until I settled my spirit, forgot about the rumors and focused on the Lord that I received a release about where to go and what to do. I had a meeting with the members of the church and asked them what they thought about having service in a community center until we found another location. They all agreed. We held service in the community center for one month.

Chapter 3 Wrestling Lessons

Never let your possessions posses you and cause you to question who you are or what you are called to do.

1. The things we experience are to make us, not break us. What have you experienced that caused you to be broken?

_____

_____

_____

_____

_____

2. The pain of yesterday should not cripple you from moving forward in the blessings of your tomorrow. List some painful situations that you allowed to take your focus off of the blessing.

_____

_____

_____

_____

_____

3. Problems allow you to encourage others to stand the tests of time. What are some testimonies you have that can relate to or bless others?

_____

_____

_____

_____

_____

Chapter 3   Wrestling Strategies

1. Stop settling for less than you desire.
   - Decide what you want, then pursue it.
   - Never lose value within yourself.
   - Recognize good and bad decisions.
   - Make good decisions a habit.

2. Don't let others stop you from pursuing your dreams.
   - Have a vision for your life and stick to it.
   - Know that people are people.
   - Stay focused on what's truly important.

3. Make a "Wish List." Then arrange the items on your wish list according to priority. Beginning with the first item, develop a game plan for accomplishing each one.

_____

_____

_____

_____

_____

_____

CHAPTER 4

A DESOLATE WRESTLE

Despite all my fasting and praying for a location to worship, I was still hurting and wrestling within myself. My wife, Edith, and one of our former members talked frequently about the faithfulness of God. They believed that no matter what comes or goes, God was going to bring us through. After all we had just gone through; I was not as focused in my faith as I should have been. It seemed as though I left a part of me in that building. Another "god" took up residence in my life: the god of worry.

One day Edith called me about a building she had seen while driving. It was a 22,000 square foot building and they were advertising 11,000 square feet available for lease. I thought this sounded great! Even better, the owner of the building was a real estate tycoon who owned more square footage of warehouse buildings than anyone else in the state of California. He was (and is) a multibillionaire known for selling buildings to a couple of non-profit organizations for one dollar.

Edith put together a proposal and asked this same former member to go with her to speak with the owner of the building. When they arrived, the secretary told them that he was out to lunch, but even so, they would need to speak with the office manager regarding any of the buildings for lease. Edith expressed very strongly her desire to speak to the owner directly. Impressed by her passion, the secretary said that although she could not schedule a meeting, they were free to contact him at the restaurant where he was having lunch. It was called The Stock Market and was not very far from their office.

When Edith and her friend arrived at The Stock Market, the restaurant was full of men in suits and ties. No other females were present, and of all the men, only one was African American. Edith told me later that they felt they were in a very awkward position. But being the focused woman she is, Edith squared her shoulders, took a deep breath and asked to be seated.

On the way to their table she looked around the restaurant, trying to identify the man they had come to see. Fortunately for her, everyone in the restaurant looked to be under the age of 40 except one grey-haired man, who seemed to be in his late 60s. Sure enough, he was the man. He sat at a table with eight other men. Edith and her friend ordered lunch and waited for the gentlemen to finish their meal.

As soon as the man stood up from the table, Edith made her way over to him, introduced herself, handed him the proposal and explained that she was asking him to donate that building to us.

"That building is worth 2.5 million dollars," he said.

"I know," Edith replied, "but we need it for ministry."

He said, "I can't donate the entire building to you, but I will give you a substantial discount on the lease."

We ended up getting six months free rent, and in the lease we would only pay $4,000.00 per month for the 11,000 square feet. When we called his office the following Monday, we found that the only catch was that we were responsible for the carpet in the area we wanted for the sanctuary. Excluding the sanctuary area, the entire building was fully carpeted. The space that was large enough for the sanctuary held 200 people and had previously been used as a storage warehouse, and therefore had needed no carpet. The offices and the classrooms were nice and set up perfectly for our school and for what we were doing in the community. We moved in and went right to work. We opened the school and the Lord began to prosper us again.

At the beginning of winter, we found that the heater did not work, and that quickly became a problem. One Sunday morning, I remember sitting in the pulpit in the midst of a cold sanctuary watching the adults and children bundled up with their coats and blankets, trying to stay warm. Everyone was maintaining faith in the vision of the church even though the heater did not work. The sanctuary was full to capacity, the presence of the Lord was strong in the service and the prophetic flow was powerful. A musician was set free from addiction that morning. He felt so blessed of God that he gave $600.00 to the offering.

After I finished preaching, I went into my office and asked God to give me my mandate for the world. The Holy Spirit responded, "Pray, preach, and prophesy." I fell on my face and worshiped Him for giving me instructions. That was the word I needed to equip me for the journey. If you humbly seek His face, God will give you the information you need to survive when faced with challenges.

We received so many testimonies of great victory after that particular service. One of them concerned my sister, who was (and is) my praise and worship leader. At that time she was having problems with her voice. She had developed nodules on her vocal cords, which the doctors attributed to stress and singing incorrectly. The only remedy was surgery to remove the nodules. After surgery she would not be able to sing for a while. On this particular Sunday when the service was so powerful, my sister was healed completely and the surgery was cancelled.

One day when we had been in the building for two months, I was out driving and on a hunch, decided to drive by our old building and see what was new. As I passed the building, I noticed that the movie theater behind it was empty. I could not believe it! I was so shocked that I immediately called Edith and told her. "You are not going to believe this." She said, "What?" I said, "The movie theater has gone out of business." My first thought was that perhaps my vision about owning the property in that area was not dead. Maybe God was giving me a second chance or a better chance. Two months earlier, the theater had been open, showing movies and popping popcorn; but now it was locked up tight. It was amazing.

I tried to make contact with the owner of the building but did not have any luck. A call to the former manager of the movie theater yielded better results. He gave me the owner's phone number. When I reached the owner at his home in Hawaii, he seemed like a very nice older man who was plainspoken and got right to the point.

"We are not a leasing company," he told me. "We only sell our buildings."

I hung up the phone thoroughly disappointed. I went to church and praised the Lord, but in my spirit I was wondering how I could get into that movie theater.

The church had the same momentum; we were experiencing growth and God was still with us. We were going forth in our new location. However, I was still trying to get the landlord to fix the heat. He said he would, but that it would take some time. Nevertheless, we continued to worship the Lord. We kept having services and fulfilling the vision in the community. Another success was our school, which incorporated grades K-12. Minister Barnes, my Assistant Pastor, resigned his job once again, this time to help me run our school. My aunt was a retired preschool teacher, and I felt so honored when she came to work for the school. One of the deacons persuaded his employer to donate six computers. Another member arranged for a donation of hundreds of books for the school's library from the Sacramento Unified School District, which also gave us desks and chairs. We had everything we needed for a successful program. It was an awesome feeling to see the school going forth and the church progressing. Part of our vision was coming to pass before my eyes.

One Sunday morning I arrived at the church early to study before everyone else showed up for prayer at 9:00. Entering the church through my office door, I noticed that my desk, the carpet, my computer, and my bookshelves were all covered with some type of powder. At first I thought it was confined to my office, but as I walked through the building, I realized I was wrong. Powder was sprayed on all of our files in the school classrooms, in the computer lab, in the school library; everywhere.

I entered Edith's office and noticed that her computer was gone, along with all of her discs with years of research and information. Edith was in the process of writing her book about prayer, and someone had come into her office and taken everything. Her entire office was also covered with this white powdery substance. I walked out, being careful not to touch anything.

After discovering the theft of Edith's computer, I called the police and waited outside for them, and for Edith and the men of the church.

When the police arrived, the news and camera crew showed up with them. As we began to walk through the building, they followed me with the camera. I pointed out some of the things that were missing, such as the computers.

When we walked into sanctuary, I received another shock. The speakers, drums and microphones were gone. I was devastated. How could this have happened? What really made me angry was when I walked on the platform and saw the organ covered in powder. That's when I began to cry; I couldn't hold it in. I had not realized until that moment when I began to cry very hard that I was in shock and very mad at whomever it was that did it. I really did not realize until now, how much sentimental value that organ had for me. Originally, it had belonged to my father, and was in his church in Reno, Nevada. In 1966, someone started a fire in the church, and my father ran in the burning building and covered the organ with a tarp so it would not get damaged. My mother gave me the organ years later.

Now, in my own church, I stood next to that same organ, which was covered with white powder. I flip the power switch, but the organ would not turn on. Empty fire extinguishers lay on the floor next to the organ. What were the odds of that? Someone had broken into the church, stolen what they wanted, then taken the fire extinguishers off the walls and vandalized the building by spraying everything, including my father's organ. I was heartbroken; and I could not hide my feelings. The news station caught my reaction on camera. After the report appeared on the evening news, we received numerous calls for donations of new organs. Grateful for all the offers, we accepted only one, which was all we needed.

Two hours after I arrived at the church, other members of the congregation began to gather for our regular time of prayer. They all had the same question: "Where are we going to have worship service today?"

I did not know. Then a thought came to my mind. "Everybody get back in your cars and follow me," I said. We drove over to the newly-closed movie theater. I wanted to show everyone what we could do if God opens the door. When we arrived, everyone got out of their cars and we stood in front of the building and prayed. Afterwards, we walked around the building three times because it was too cold and the building was too large to go around seven times (as the Israelites did at Jericho). While walking around the building, we felt the power of God. We also praised Him for the vision and believed Him to bring it to pass.

Then I began to speak into people's lives as if I was inside a building. We prayed for a woman who was sick, and she was healed right there outside that empty movie theater. We were all excited about what God was doing in that parking lot. Not only were our regular members blessed, but a visitor who had come along with us from our vandalized building wanted to join with us right there on the spot without our even being in a church building.

After the service we went back to our building and dealt with the problem. During that time in Sacramento there were several churches and synagogues that had experienced vandalism, burglaries, and in some cases, arson. The police classified these acts of violence as hate crimes.

I was amazed by the love and support we received from the community after that horrible experience. I wondered why the perpetrators didn't just steal the equipment and leave. Why did they have to vandalize the church and cause so much damage? Edith had a brand new color copy machine in her office and they sprayed the extinguisher all throughout until it was useless. Even after everything was cleaned up and put back together, I still felt violated and really did not want to stay in the building. I kept calling the theater owners about the possibility of leasing the movie theater.

I was discouraged by the lack of response, but through prayer the Lord encourage me to try again. So I called one last time and left a message on the voicemail. I asked the owner to consider a lease/option and stated my terms. Two days later I received a return call in which the owner agreed to our terms for the lease/option. I was astonished; I could not believe that we were finally going to have an opportunity to do something great for the Lord at this level. When I called the owner of the building that had been vandalized, he understood my concerns and allowed us to get out of the lease with no problem or penalty.

After we moved out of the building I remembered an experience I had had about a month prior to the burglary. I was at the church and a preacher stopped by my office and said, "God wants you to tell Him how you really feel about the situation that took place before you moved into this building." He told me to tell Him if I was angry, sad or hurt. He said God wanted me to let Him know how I really felt. I went to God in prayer and told Him that I was angry and hurt, because every time we started growing, we got hit with some kind of crisis and had to move. I was also angry because my dad was deceased and unavailable to help me. My brother-in-law was doing fine in the church that my father founded, and I was just plain angry and hurt because I was the one who seemed to always come up short.

The following week I attended a revival in the city of Vallejo, California. The guest speaker was the late Pastor Nathan Simmons. He preached with such passion and conviction that people were really blessed. When he made an appeal for the altar call; I did not go, but I did get on my knees. I asked God to show me my hurt. And when God revealed it to me, I cried for two days. I went home and immediately called my sister and brother-in-law, asking them to forgive me for allowing my hurt to stop them from moving forward. I did not realize that after years of going forth in ministry, I was still hurt.

My brother-in-law became the pastor of my father's church in 1985, after my father passed; I was 15 years old at the time. Nine years later, we all thought my brother-in-law was going to move to a new church and that I would take over my father's church. It did not happen the way we thought, which was no fault of my brother-in-law. However, when he did not get the church he was expecting, that also meant I could not get my father's church either. For the next three months, I fasted and prayed. I never realized I carried that hurt over into my ministry when I started my own church in 1995.

After the church was vandalized, the wound that I thought was healed re-opened. I learned that there may be times in your life when you think you are fine, but until God reveals the problem, you cannot be healed. If it's not revealed it cannot be healed. After I was healed, I could move on to receive what God had for me. Yet even during this time of personal growth and advancement, I opened the door of my mind for another false "god" to take root in my consciousness: misunderstanding.

Chapter 4   Wrestling Lessons

Even though you may experience depression, disappointment or loss on your journey, do not allow it to deter you from your dreams.

1. If God has given you a vision and you believe it, it will come to pass. What are some things God has given you to do that you have allowed disappointments to keep you from doing?

   _____

   _____

   _____

   _____

   _____

   _____

2. Don't be afraid to go after things God has placed in your heart. What causes you to be afraid to go after your vision?

   _____

   _____

   _____

   _____

   _____

   _____

3. Keep going and growing. Remember, there is no such thing as failure until you stop. List some things you have a desire to accomplish. What are some specific actions you can take to see them through?

   _____

   _____

   _____

   _____

   _____

   _____

Chapter 4   Wrestling Strategies

1. What happens if certain methods don't work the first time?
   - Try different methods in the future.
   - Try, and then try again; try it differently; try until you get it right; whatever you do, just keep trying.

2. Get rid of all internal conflicts that cause fear, anger and hurt, which limit you from becoming successful.
   - Reflect on good times you had in your life.
   - Know that you are significant to others.
   - Focus, focus, focus.

3. Write down the "pros and cons" of the goals you are trying to accomplish.

   _____

   _____

   _____

   _____

   _____

   _____

4. Write down what you need to give up and who you need to forgive in order to move forward in your life.

   _____

   _____

   _____

   _____

   _____

   _____

CHAPTER 5

THE SILENT
WRESTLE

Two days before Easter Sunday we received the keys to the movie theater. We had so much work to do to get the building ready for Easter Service. My assistant, Pastor Barnes, Jim Allen, Don White, and all the ministers and deacons got together and worked day and night. By Sunday morning we had everything ready for the worship service. It was amazing to see this vision come to pass. During that time we had met in the old Oshman's building next door, I had told the church that one day we would have service in the movie theater building. Now, one year later, we did.

I was extremely grateful to the Lord for entrusting us with such an awesome project. Everyone was excited about the opportunity to purchase this 22,000 square foot building. There were five individual theaters, a large snack bar in the lobby area and large restrooms. We put a lot of work into transforming the movie theater into a worship atmosphere. We converted the screen rooms upstairs into classrooms for the school. We removed the curtains from the walls, painted the walls, removed hundreds of theater seats from the ground to make a multipurpose room, and placed a platform in the main sanctuary. When it was all done, we were exhausted but very enthused about working for the Lord in this new facility. Speaking the prophecy that we would worship in this building at a time when the movie theater was still up and running was my act of faith. Producing it was God's manifestation. I literally experienced feeling my faith moving God.

During this season everything was going well for the church. My family was suffering and lacking in certain areas, however, because I sacrificed my offerings and took no salary. My thought was that I did not want to receive any money from the church because the expense of repairing the building was so great. After all we had been through; I wanted the people to see the blessings of the Lord. Whenever I did receive a love offering, it was never enough to pay my rent or even my car note. As a result, every now and then we had to move to another house or pray for favor to get through those difficult times.

In any case, I sacrificed for the church and for the Kingdom of God, yet people in the community still talked about me and said negative things about the church, my ministry, and my family. Some people called us the "mobile church" because we moved so often, while others accused me of not taking care of my family. Some even said I was moving too fast. I thought people would be more apt to celebrate the fact that I was working hard for the church and giving back to help people. For years I had heard about pastors and evangelists who took money from the church to pay their own bills and let the church go lacking. They were merely in ministry for self-gain. That is why I was shocked to hear people talking negatively about me when I made sacrifices for the church. I learned that as long as I prayed, the things other people said about me did not affect me.

One month after we moved into the movie theater, something happened that *did* affect me. One day, completely out of the blue, one of my faithful deacons who had been with me for two years stopped by my office and resigned. He just said, "Pastor, it's time for me to go."

"Go where?" I asked "Are you coming back?"

He replied, "No, it's time to go."

"Okay," I said, completely bewildered.

He left the church, just like that, with no explanation. I began wrestling within myself, wondering why he had left. I could not sleep for three days. He had been a good church member, reliable, faithful in attendance and in giving. People come and go, but what hit me the hardest about his departure was that I had no clue as to his reasons for doing so. We did not fall out or have any disagreements that I was aware of. Finally, someone told me that this deacon was upset with one of the other pastors in the church. When I heard that, I realized that it was indeed his time to leave.

Embracing Change

Change is the law of life. And those who look only to the past or present are certain to miss the future.

-John F. Kennedy

One thing I learned is that every member who comes through the doors is on an assignment for a certain time, some longer than others. Members have actually taught me many things during their time in the ministry, some more valuable than others, but lessons nonetheless, and I will treasure them for a lifetime. Another thing I learned is that people join churches for many reasons. Some join to encourage others, and some join to *be* encouraged. Some people join for the notoriety of being able to say that they attend a great church. In some ways it doesn't matter why people join or how many people join. What matters is learning. I learned to be faithful in the work with those with whom the Lord had entrusted me. As Simon Peter counseled church leaders:

> *Feed the flock of God which is among you, taking the oversight thereof, not by constraint, but willingly; not for filthy lucre, but of a ready mind; Neither as being lords over God's heritage, but being ensamples to the flock.* (1 Peter 5:2-3)

Eight months after we moved into the movie theater, I received a call that my brother-in-law had resigned from my father's church in Reno. He had gone independent and started his own church downtown. It was a shock to the entire community as well as to the Church of God in Christ in the State of Nevada. I called the district superintendent to schedule a meeting because my mother wanted to know what he had in mind for the church. She also wanted to express her feelings about the church because she was the co-founder and had a great love for the people. She did not want to see the church suffer because my brother-in-law had a vision of his own. He believed that God had given him a vision to pioneer his own organization. Rumors were flying as to who would be the next pastor of the church. Different people were calling from all over expressing interest in the position. I was not one of them. I never called the Bishop seeking to become the pastor of that church; I was too busy trying to settle and establish the one I had.

My brother-in-law joined us for the meeting with the district superintendent so that he could express his feelings about the situation. After he was finished, my mother spoke, and as I sat there and thought about what each of them had to say, I really felt that my mother had a heart that cared deeply for the church. Suddenly, and before I could catch myself, I blurted out to the superintendent, "Why don't you and I take the church until we find a permanent pastor."

He said, "No. I'm fine right here at my local church and I don't want to do that."

Then I just dug myself in deeper. "I'll take the church," I said.

The superintendent said he would talk to the Bishop and get his approval first. In the meantime, I continued working hard in the church in Sacramento.

Feel the Fear and Do Away with It

The Bishop called a meeting with the members of my father's church to get their opinion about me and the situation. I was not in the meeting, but I was told it was not favorable. After hearing from the members, the Bishop called me into the sanctuary and presented me to the members by saying, "His father would have wanted him to be the pastor if he was still alive. This is the right decision for the church."

Immediately, one of the long-time members I had known and loved all my life got up and walked out, extremely upset. Others stayed long enough to see what I was going to say and do, but they ended up leaving the church altogether. When the meeting was over and everyone was gone, another one of the ladies that I loved dearly came to me with tears in her eyes and said, "You just want your father's church."

"What?" I said, uncertain that I had understood her correctly.

She said, "I was told that your brother-in-law wanted a severance pay, your mother wanted monthly payments, and you wanted your father's church."

I could not believe what I was hearing.

> *We come this way but once. We can either tip-toe through life and hope that we get to death without being too badly bruised or we can live a full, complete life achieving our goals and realizing our wildest dreams.*
>
> -Bob Proctor

There were rumors that if I became the pastor, I would bring all my members from Sacramento and put them in the leadership positions. This was why everyone was so upset. I praise God that I had prepared myself while waiting for a response from the Bishop. I expressed my thoughts in writing, and also created a spreadsheet showing all the current leaders and the positions they held in the church in Reno.

When this dear lady said these things to me, I opened my computer and showed her the vision that the Lord had given me for the leadership of the church. When she saw her name and others in the same positions they were already in, she calmed down. I told her I would never fire everyone from their positions. Although these positions were not paid, they were important to the people. I promised that I would not make any drastic decisions for at least five years. I expressed to her our love for the church and that I would never do anything to hurt them. For me, this was literally a dream come true; I was back home in Reno. God had given me the vision of how to do it and I was ready to do ministry.

Complete the Past to Embrace the Future

> *None of us can change our yesterdays, but all of us can change our tomorrows.*
>
> -Colin Powell

It was December 1999, five years and eight months after I received my healing from the silent wrestle about not getting my father's church, when my brother-in-law was released to do what he felt God had called him to do. This taught me a valuable lesson: what God has for you is for *you*. When God's hand is on you, He will not allow you to get out of His hedge until you are ready to move forward and receive the promise. I thought my silent wrestle was over five years earlier, when I received my healing. I didn't realize that it was only the end of that round. Now the bell rang, and I was back in the middle of the wrestling ring.

Six months had passed and I was enjoying the journey. I had a vision to unify the churches; I even changed the name of the Reno church so both locations were now The Greater Harvest. This was the third name change since my father had died, and to my surprise, the members openly accepted the name change. I set a speaking schedule for both churches for the next six months so that everyone knew who was speaking and when. I even started an 8:00am service in Sacramento so I could preach early on Sunday morning then get in my car and drive two hours over the mountains to Reno and preach at the 11:00am service. Rain, sleet or snow, I was ready to do the work of the Lord. In all those years of traveling, I can remember only one time when tire chains were required to drive on the mountain. It was an amazing experience and the Lord was really speaking to me through His Word. People were being encouraged and blessed. We had a church cook-out in Reno; the men from Sacramento went to Reno and painted the church; Sacramento and Reno went out witnessing together in Reno. All in all, things were great.

The Sacramento church was growing and we were still working on the building. One day the fire department came to the church to do an inspection and complained about the fire equipment. They wanted us to bring the equipment up to code, and it was going to cost over $50,000.00. We tried to get it grandfathered because it was on older building, but due to its size, being over 20,000 square feet, they did not want to make an exception.

This was very discouraging, especially because we were trying to exercise our option to purchase the theater. We suffered a further setback when our loan was approved only for 80% of the amount we needed. We presented it to the owner with the request that they finance the other 20% for two years, but they were unwilling to do this. They said no. What they did do was a miracle in itself; they allowed us to stay in the building rent free until they sold it, which was a blessing. Unfortunately, this meant we had to find *another* building to house our church. I was very disappointed.

> *As long as you don't forgive, who and whatever it is will occupy rent-free space in your mind.*
>
> -Isabelle Holland

In the meantime, we continued working in the community. I tried to keep my head above what I was going through and continued to walk in faith. This was very hard because I was going through a similar situation in my own life. I was also trying to exercise my option to purchase the house we lived in. I went in with a two-year lease/option and, oddly enough, I needed the owner of the house to carry back a very small amount, just as I needed for the church building. He could not do it because it would have put him in another tax bracket.

I was trying to provide stability for both my family and the church, but things were not coming together. The pressure was so great, I felt like I was going to snap, but I didn't. I continued to preach the Word. People were being saved, delivered and set free. God was leading people to join the church. Our telecast was very successful. Edith and I would stand outside the church and record our telecast for the week and people would attend in great numbers. Acts Full Gospel Church from Oakland, California brought a charter busload of people who went witnessing with us in the community, and it was wonderful.

Transform Your Inner Critic into Your Inner Coach

> *Don't believe everything you hear – even in your own mind.*
>
> -Daniel G. Amen, MD

One morning not long after this, I woke up, went into the bathroom, and started to cry. I cried so hard that I could not stop. I did not know if I was having a nervous breakdown, or what. Edith ran in the bathroom, grabbed my head in both hands, and said, "John! John! John! It's going to be alright! Stop crying; all is well!"

Suddenly it was like God came and called me back to reality. I got myself together and came out of the bathroom. I had to press my way through that situation, because even though the Lord was blessing our services, we were still meeting in a building with a "For Sale" sign in front of it. I found it humiliating, because potential buyers were walking through the building almost every week. It was a lot of pressure for a 30 year-old pastor who woke up every day asking the Lord, "Where do we go from here?" In my subconscious mind I was dealing with the "gods" of pride and entitlement. I thought that because of my faithfulness, God owed this to me.

A man is literally what he thinks. -James Allen

Today, it astonishes me to look back on my experiences during this season in my life. I was the leader, yet I was so confused. I was trying to follow God, even as the people followed me. My problem was that I had no idea where God was leading me. I was the pastor of two churches in two different cities, which was amazing enough all by itself.

Then the hammer dropped twice in the same day. The owner of the movie theater called to tell me he had just sold the building. I had barely gotten over that news when the owner of our house told me we could not extend the lease because he wanted to sell it.

The next morning we woke up to the sound of a tow truck towing my car away. I ran out the house and showed the tow truck driver the receipt for the car payment. I called the finance company and told them we made our payment. The finance company confirmed that they had received our payment, but said it was too late. That really did not bother me too much; I just went to the car lot and bought a nicer, newer one.

The issue of our car was resolved, but we still had to move out of the house and the movie theater building. By this time I was sick and tired of the frequent transitions and moves.

Let me pause right here to give you some understanding. As a young preacher you can easily become overwhelmed with trying to please people. Even though I was uncertain, Almighty God is never confused. He says what He means and means what He says. The denomination I was part of allowed you to be on your own and did not provide the resources you needed to provide for your church the way most other denominations did. Looking back, I now believe that some of the transitions I went through were to help other leaders, pastors and business owners understand the importance of how to transition and how to stay faithful even when life is crazy and things are chaotic. I thank God for the opportunities that I experienced in these areas of my life. They caused me to be a better leader for others because I could understand what they go through. Sometimes God will allow you to go through silence to see if you will trust Him, even when you cannot hear Him.

Chapter 5   Wrestling Lessons

When you are struggling with a silent wrestle, you have become disconnected from people. When this happens, you are in need of connection. There are six basic human needs, and you need to address at least one or more (ideally all six) in order to bring healing and renewal.

1. The six (6) basic human needs are:
    a. Certainty.
    b. Variety.
    c. Significance.
    d. Connection and love.
    e. Growth.
    f. Contribution.

Which of these do you feel you need the most? Why?

_____

_____

_____

_____

2. When you are dealing with:
    a. Frustration.
    b. Anger.
    c. Resentment.
    d. Rage.

It is because you need Significance and Certainty. What situations are you going through that cause you to feel this way?

_____

_____

_____

_____

3. When you are dealing with:
    a. Depression.
    b. Loneliness.
    c. Sadness.
    d. Being Misunderstood.

It's because you are in need of Connection and Variety. What situations are you going through that cause you to feel this way?

_____

_____

_____

_____

_____

_____

Chapter 5 Wrestling Strategies

1. Write down some of the things you wrestle with. Find out what you lack and then try to develop a model.

_____

_____

_____

_____

_____

1. Change your perspective and try to see as God sees:
    a. About yourself .
    b. About your success.
    c. About your career.
    d. About your ministry.

_____

_____

_____

_____

1. Change your patterns:
    a. Regarding your conflicting rules.
        (Rules that conflict with goals bring confusion.)
    b. Regarding your approach to problems.

_____

_____

_____

_____

1. Regarding your daily action:
   a. Visualize your day.
   b. Visualize your goals, visions and dreams.
   c. Make affirmations.
   d. Pray and meditate.
   e. Have an attitude of praise and worship.
   f. Take action.

_____

_____

_____

_____

_____

CHAPTER 6

WRESTLING
BETWEEN TWO CITIES

*In all thy ways acknowledge him, and he shall direct
thy paths.* (Proverbs 3:6)

In the midst of trying to locate a new home for the church as well
as a home for my family; I continued to pray and consult God about the
future direction of both churches. I have always prayed and acknowl-
edged God, requesting wisdom in making decisions; especially when
they impacted the church. After I was officially installed into the church
in Reno, I leased a condominium, where my family and I stayed when
we were in town.

One day I decided to stay in Reno for an extended period in order
to seek God. While I was there, I consecrated myself by fasting and praying for 21 days, fervently seeking God's direction for both churches. I
wanted the church members to know that I was following the leading
of the Lord rather than my own agenda. Some members wanted me to
have a meeting as soon as I became the pastor, but I declined, saying that
we were going to go to God first. After the 21 days, I called a meeting
in a restaurant at the Reno Nugget Hotel, where I shared the plan that I
believed the Lord had given me.

I laid out the offices and those who were to be leaders in the different departments. I did not make many changes, keeping most of the
same leaders in place. The changes I did make were necessary because the
members in those positions had either resigned or joined other churches
or both. I explained that I would attend the church in Reno every 2nd and

4th Sunday; the church in Sacramento every 1st & 3rd Sundays and one of the services during the week. We ate dinner and then concluded the meeting. I did not feel led to have the meeting at the church, as had been done for over 30 years. Instead, I wanted to bring in a new perspective and introduce them to the way I was going to lead. It turned out to be a very good meeting.

I was at a pivotal point in my life. After I was appointed the pastor of the church in Reno, the Bishop appointed me district superintendent over Northern Nevada. I was the youngest superintendent in the history of the State of Nevada. In the Church of God in Christ, a district consists of a group of churches that has monthly fellowship services and then a large conference once a year. I was both humbled and honored, because my father had been the district superintendent years before me. It felt like a dream, but it was also scary because I knew that my father's shoes were much too large for me to fill. But with God's help I was willing to do whatever the Lord wanted. I was amazed at how God literally orchestrated my destiny.

Road Blocks

What we think or what we know or what we believe is, in the end, of little consequence. The only consequence is what we do.

-John Ruskin

All my life, the Northern District had been an awesome district and now I was a part of it as a pastor, or so I thought. As soon as I was appointed the pastor of the church in Reno, all the other pastors in the Northern District pulled out of the Nevada Ecclesiastical Jurisdiction in order to form their own jurisdiction. They did not want to continue under the leadership of the current Bishop, who was over the entire state of Nevada. After they made that decision, people tried to encourage me to join forces with them. I kindly stated my position and let them know that I was going to remain with our current jurisdictional Bishop; the same Bishop, I might add, who had appointed me to the church in the first place. The jurisdictional Bishop is appointed by the national organization and represents the church in state affairs. You must be approved by the General Board of the Church of God in Christ in order to operate in such form.

I had been a part of this denomination all of my life and knew how it operated. I love our denomination and would never jeopardize the church or its members in order to advance someone else's vision. That is, unless the Lord gave me permission. I prayed about it and the Lord told me not to leave the jurisdiction. I stood my ground and was widely criticized for doing so. I received continuous pressure from the members of our church, who eventually began rebelling against me. Even after the group of pastors presented their case before the General Board and were denied year after year, people continued to turn on me. I kept finding myself with a fight on my hands. Since I was the new kid on the block, it was not even my fight. I had nothing to do with the decisions that were being made. Even after this group of pastors was instructed by the late Presiding Bishop, G.E. Patterson on numerous occasions to "cease and desist," they continued to ridicule me and talk about me because I would not join their efforts.

I was forced to change the name of the District to Greater Northern Nevada District because the former Superintendent still used that name and continued to function with the former district pastors. I only had one church in my district, and it was mine. I was determined more than ever to make it work with the help of the Lord.

My first district conference was in March, four months after I became the pastor and superintendent. The local pastors boycotted me; they did not want to support my conference. So I called in friends and allies from California, and we had a great time in the Lord. The church was filled; the locals would not have been able to get inside even if they had come. Attendance was great every night. The speakers were powerful and the Lord blessed the fellowship.

I just do not hang around anybody that I don't want to be with, period. For me, that's been a blessing, and I can stay positive. I hang around people who are happy, who are growing, who want to learn, who don't mind saying sorry or thank you… and [are] having a fun time.

-John Assaraf

It was a lonely time in my life, but I was so grateful to the Lord for smiling on us. The loneliness only set in when I thought about the other pastors in the district, whom I considered my brothers. They were all older than me, and I had known the majority of them all my life. Some of them had been mentored by my father years ago. When I returned to Reno to pastor his church, I thought it was going to be like the good old days. I really was looking forward to it. I hoped that being in Reno would help comfort some of the hurts or fill some of the voids in my life from the struggles I dealt with in Sacramento.

Paying the Price

You have to believe in yourself when no one else does. That's what makes you a winner.

-Venus Williams

The challenges in Sacramento caused the members there to start doubting me when I committed to the church in Reno. They started receiving pressure from their family members, who told them, "Your pastor is going to move to Reno and shut the church down in Sacramento." Some of the members thought I was going to abandon them. Rumors got even worse when we moved out of the movie theater, because I couldn't find a location appropriate enough for worship. The members agreed to have services at the Governors Inn Hotel for a couple of months.

When I finally did find a location, it was on the other side of town. The building had been a church previously and all in all was pretty nice.

It was fully furnished with a PA system, microphone equipment, 200 chairs, an organ and a clear podium. The landlord said that we could use the offices, the sanctuary, and the additional space for the children's ministry. There was also an option for us to purchase the building if desired. The only downside to the location was that it was upstairs. However, the landlord also told us he was working on installing an elevator, so we thought, "This can work!"

When I took all the members to see the place, they all liked it and agreed that we should move there. The landlord said he would get the contract ready for us, but in the mean time we could move in. Everybody was energized, and I said to myself, "Here we go again!"

A short time before we were to make this move, my cousin was talking on the phone with her former classmate, professional football player Marshall Faulk. When she told him the challenges our church had faced that year, he told her that he wanted to help us. She mailed him the videotape of the news report that was recorded after the vandalism at our former location. Mr. Faulk contacted a charitable organization and asked them to team up with him and match his gift to help us. One Sunday morning, the organization attended our service at the Governors Inn Hotel and presented us with a check for $14,000.00; $7000.00 from the organization and $7,000.00 from Marshall Faulk.

What an encouragement this was for us, especially since we were on the verge of another move. In addition to the move, the donation also paid for new church equipment that was much needed. The Lord seemed to be smiling on us again. I even found a house to lease on the same side of town, which shortened my travel time to Reno. The house was 30 minutes from Sacramento and 1 ½ hours from Reno. It was a large two-story home that was very unique, situated on one acre of land. The only thing that separated us from the neighbors was a large septic tank in the middle of the back yard. The neighbors, however, were acres away, so it was very peaceful there.

The main entrance to the house was on the second floor, which contained the kitchen, living room, master bedroom, two bathrooms and two smaller bedrooms. Downstairs, similar to a basement, held the kid's game room, the family room, three additional bedrooms, one bathroom, a laundry room and a kitchenette.

Edith was pregnant with our eighth child and was in her last trimester. When she was tired after our evening services, she was grateful we did not live far from the church. One night only a couple of months after moving into the house, we arrived home from church and everyone had to use the bathroom; all three bathrooms were occupied at the same time. When the children were finished, they came upstairs to my room and we all watched television together.

A short time later, we heard a weird sound coming from downstairs. Edith ran downstairs to investigate and found that sewage was backing up in the bathtub. We called the landlord, who explained that the septic tank was old and needed to be pumped out. He sent someone over to turn the water off and scheduled someone to come the next morning to pump out the septic tank. He said that should take care of the problem because the tank only needed to be pumped out every six months.

Two days later, we heard the sound again. This time the kids came running upstairs screaming. We went to check it out and the entire downstairs was flooding. Water was pouring through the pipes in the walls, the toilet was overflowing, and fluid was backing up into the bathtub, the laundry room, and the sink in the kitchenette. We turned the water off but the flooding did not stop. By the time we went back upstairs to call the landlord, the kitchen sink and both bathrooms upstairs were backing up. I immediately got my family out of the house and we went to a hotel.

Using a Bad Experience to My Advantage

Only those who dare to fail can ever achieve greatly.
-Robert F. Kennedy

When we returned, there were people everywhere, working inside and outside the house. People from the health department were there, and contractors were removing all the sheetrock from the walls downstairs. Everyone was walking around in protective suits with gas masks on their faces, sterilizing the house. Everything was contaminated. The smell was so bad it made Edith very sick. They took all of our furniture out; Edith's new family room furniture, the children's beds, the dressers, the dining room table in the kitchenette, the washer and dryer, and all of my kids' clothes and toys and threw them away outside in a large dumpster. It was absolutely horrible.

Edith was devastated, and I was frustrated and tired because we had to move again, after only two months in the house. This time we did not have very much to move. Even though the upstairs did not get wet, everything was contaminated from the smell, so we did not want any of the furniture. I told Edith that I would buy her all new furniture, and she just cried. We gathered what we could from the house, which basically was clothing and the items that were still packed in the garage. We rented storage up the street and then drove to Reno for our weekly service.

When we returned to Sacramento, the owner of the church building finally gave us a copy of the lease. After we were in the building for a while, he called me and said we could only have services at night and on certain days. This was something he had not told us before, and it was not in the contract. He waited until we moved in and then rented out the one office space that we were not using. Their office hours conflicted with our daily prayer schedule.

I went along with it for two or three months, but it hindered our ministry. The schedule conflict was not the only problem; the owner had not received the permit to install the elevator, and the older saints were having trouble getting up the stairs. I went back to the landlord and told him that I wanted to get out of the lease. When I had stated all of my reasons, he agreed.

Before we moved out of that location, I ran into the man who had been the pastor of the previous church to lease the building. He said that all the chairs, the organ, the and sound equipment belonged to him, but he would sell them to us if we were interested. I told him we certainly were interested, and he sold everything to us for a very reasonable price. Sometimes God will lead you to a place just to give you a blessing.

What Others Think about You...
Is None of Your Business

Every time the church moved I received knowledge or some type of instruction from God. People have talked about how often the church change location and how frequently my family moved from one house to another, but they will never really know the pain and suffering my family experienced. I had seven children at the time; two were at home and five were attending a Christian school. One day my oldest daughter came home from school very upset. She was a freshman in high school and one of her classmates asked her where she went to church. When she said, "Tabernacle of Praise Center," the classmate replied, "Oh, the mobile church?"

That is how I found out that I was being talked about by the children and their parents in Sacramento. The thing I did not understand was how I was being talked about by the people in Reno whom I had known all my life. As a child, I fellowshipped at their homes and now they looked at me as if they did not even know me. To add to my distress, my own members in Reno started saying, "We don't want a part-time pastor."

I had gotten used to being talked about in Sacramento, but I was hurt when the people in Reno had bad things to say because I knew those people. Later, I realized that they were hurt too. They had felt abandoned when my brother-in-law left them to start another church. What happened was that he had a meeting with the young people in the church and announced to them that he was leaving. But the older saints said, "He didn't invite us to go." Not that they would have gone; they just wanted the courtesy of an invitation. Sometimes ministry seems selfish when you are trying to be obedient to the voice of God. People assume that pastors think only about themselves and their own feelings, and this misunderstanding can cause resentment among the saints.

The significant problems we face cannot be solved by the same level of thinking that created them.

-Albert Einstein

That's what happened to Jesus. The religious leaders became furious with Jesus. They murdered Him because He showed compassion on the people who were not yet converted, such as the woman in John chapter 8 who was caught in adultery. The religious leaders brought her to Jesus in an attempt to trick Him into saying something by which they could accuse Him of breaking the religious law. Jesus simply said to them, "He that is without sin among you, let him first cast a stone at her" (John 8:7b).

We have murdered people too, maybe not on a cross, but with our mouths, our looks, and even our lack of respect for leadership. It's easy to say what my brother-in-law should have, or could have done, but he didn't have the "how-to" book for pastors. I believe if you are a leader, you must lead or get out of the way!

Just Keep On Going

The members in Sacramento agreed to go back to the Governors Inn Hotel for our services while we looked for a building again. Edith and I moved into a brand new house. It had just been built, no one had ever lived there, and it didn't have a septic system. What a relief! Two days after we moved in, Edith went into labor. That day we had our eighth and final child, a girl. Two weeks after having the baby, Edith told me that she wasn't strong enough yet to find us another building to worship in. I told her to rest and not to worry about it. If I was married to any other woman, she probably would have divorced me long ago. In fact, if *I* was married to myself, *I* would have left me a long time ago!

A few days later I went to Reno. While I was gone, Edith got out of bed and found us a church building the same day. When she called me with the news, I asked her what she was doing out of bed. She said God had told her where to go, and when she got there, the building was vacant. We signed the contract, got the keys, moved in, and had church the following Sunday. Like our previous location, it was formerly a church, so everyone was familiar with the location. We immediately started planning a prophetic conference, which was a great blessing to the people.

As I continued to go to Reno every 2nd & 4th Sunday, one of my assistant pastors Glen Clinton drove me back and forth. Eventually he began to go to Reno every Sunday to play the organ. He did that for two years, and I was so grateful. I have known him for a total of fifteen years. Growing up with eight sisters, and I being the only boy, he was like the brother I never had. We were a blessing to each other in many ways.

After he and I started going to Reno, I began to notice a difference in the attitudes of the leaders in Sacramento on the 2nd & 4th Sundays. They would drag in late and start the services late. There was no order when I wasn't there. I called a prayer meeting because murmurs of rebellion were growing. After a three-day consecration, God brought change to the minds of the members and order to the church. It was an experience I will never forget. The members started acting like children when their parents left the house; they would slack off and throw a party. I had to make sure the leaders were staying focused on the vision, so the members who were following them would do the same.

In the beginning, preaching in Reno was also relatively challenging. In order to let me know she didn't like the fact that I was there, one of the members would close her eyes when I preached. There were spectators who came to the church just to see what I was going to do. For the first year, I just preached. Some said I preached very well. They said I sounded like my father, whom they loved. I guess that's why they could put up listening to me. I was fifteen years old when my father died, so unfortunately I didn't have the opportunity to learn a lot about preaching from him. The things I did learn from him were nuggets of wisdom from statements he made.

I remember him telling us about the time he asked his father to teach him how to drive. His father (my grandfather) replied, "After watching me all this time, you should know how to drive. Sit here behind the wheel and drive." So the day I gave my oldest son his minister's license, I told the church "Come back tonight, because Minister Wynn is going to preach." I told them this same story about my father wanting to drive, and then said, "After watching me all this time, he should know how to preach." That night he spoke and it was a very good message. I was proud of him and honored that the Lord allowed me to be there to experience it with him. I wish I had the opportunity to work with my father; he was a great man, not just in the church but in the community and in business as well. It is because I didn't have that privilege that I decided to allow my children, at a very young age, to enjoy the journey of ministry, business, and community with me.

When I became the pastor of my father's church, I did not change very much. I just preached the Word. Some of the members often questioned me as to why I wouldn't go with the Northern District. I would ask, "Go with them where? They have not been approved to be a jurisdiction by the national church." I got a lot of criticism, but I had to stand my ground and be obedient to the voice of God. It was hard, because I loved those pastors. I had known them all my life, but what they were engaged in was not my fight. I had enough on my plate battling two churches in two different cities.

Chapter 6   Wrestling Lessons

Here are some questions you need to consider when dealing with opportunities.

1. When you are building a business, family, career, ministry or a relationship; you have to beware of toxic people. Do you have toxic people in your life? If you do, list them and get them out of your life.

_____

_____

_____

_____

_____

2. When people are close to you who can't see your vision, it is important that you protect the vision. What are some visions you have allowed negative people to stop you from going after?

_____

_____

_____

_____

_____

3. Do you know who you are? Do you value yourself? If not, think of some things you can do to help you change your perspective of yourself.

_____

_____

_____

_____

_____

Chapter 6   Wrestling Strategies

1. Write down some positive things about yourself and speak those things daily.
    - I am an overcomer and my faith is changing my circumstances.
    - What I see now is only temporary.
    - NO weapon formed against me shall prosper.

2. How can you benefit from those who don't believe?
    - Use their negative words to push you into your future.
    - Remember that "all things work together for the good of them who love the Lord and who are the called according to His purpose". (Romans 8:28)

3. What you link your pain to and what you link your pleasure to shapes your destiny.
    - If you focus on your painful experiences, you will allow it to stop you.
    - Learn to focus on the things that brought you pleasure (achievements, good friends and family, etc.).
    - If you use pain as a stepping stone, you will be able to help others through theirs.

CHAPTER 7

TICKETS TO A WRESTLING MATCH

Fight the good fight of faith, lay hold on eternal life, whereunto thou art also called, and hast professed a good profession before many witnesses. (1 Timothy 6:12)

I kept on fighting the good fight of faith. We started another building project campaign in Sacramento called, "Hand Me Another Brick." Part of the campaign plan included organizing a banquet. The fundraising committee told the church how many tickets we needed to sell in order to make a good profit. They issued tickets to the members and everyone committed to purchase at least two tickets and try to sell two others. Edith prepared a banquet for one hundred and fifty people. I asked my Jurisdictional Prelate, Bishop J.W. Macklin, to be my guest speaker, and he agreed. Edith and the committee rented a beautiful banquet room and worked diligently to make the banquet a success. We advertized well in advance and people began to RSVP and many others said they would pay at the door. On the night of the event, everything was exquisite; the decorations beautiful and the food looked very inviting. We were prepared for one hundred and fifty people. Edith and her staff had done an awesome job.

By the time Bishop Macklin and his wife arrived, we only had thirty people in attendance. People kept calling with excuses why they could not come, and only two of my own family members showed up. One of my sisters blamed Edith for the poor attendance. I was so frustrated, I am sorry to say, that I blamed her too. She and I had a pretty heated conversation backstage just before she was to walk on the stage to speak. She

93

was not crying out of disappointment because so few people attended; she did not care about that. She just said, "It's their loss, not mine! I am not going to blame myself because of uncommitted people who always make excuses of why they do not support you. I worked hard and I am going to enjoy every minute of it and I don't care what any of your sisters' say." Edith was crying because I was blaming her for the poor turnout.

Sold Out

> *You must take personal responsibility. You cannot change the circumstances, the seasons, or the wind but you can change yourself.*
>
> -Jim Rohn

That night Edith showed me what kind of woman she was. She wiped her face, dried her eyes and walked on that stage to speak as if our conversation never happened. She started off by saying, "God is going to bless us; we are not defeated and we are going to do everything that God has given us to do." She continued speaking about the vision and our plans for the church. That was a defining moment in my life. We had been married eleven years and I had never witnessed this side of her before. That night I saw a woman of power, hope and strength, a woman who believed in me even when my own family did not. When my family told me not to go forth, she told me I could do all things through Christ who strengthens me. That was a powerful moment for me.

After Edith finished, Bishop Macklin preached as if that banquet room was full. I was encouraged to go on a little further to see what the end was going to be. I apologized to Edith for taking my frustrations out on her. That night I saw a woman of excellence that went beyond people.

Preparing for an Opportunity

> *Difficulties are opportunities to better things; they are stepping-stones to greater experience...when one door closes,*

another always opens; as natural law it has to, to balance.
                                          -Brian Adams

Edith and I went to Las Vegas one January for the Nevada Jurisdictional Workers and Leaders Conference. The night we arrived we were a little late because our flight was delayed. I went up to the pulpit, but Edith did not want to sit up close, so she sat all the way in the back of the church. Bishop Felton Smith was already speaking. As soon as Edith sat down, Bishop Smith told her to stand up. He told her, "Lift your hands to the Lord and repeat after me. 'I am a millionaire and from this day forward, January 15th, I will never be broke again.'" Later that night in our hotel room, I said the Edith, "Let's pray. If God is going to bless you to be a millionaire, we need to know what type of business we need to start." After we prayed, I told her we needed to get a business license for a desktop publishing company. She was already doing that kind of work for people anyway.

Take the first step in faith. You don't have to see the whole staircase; just take the first step.
                                     -Martin Luther King Jr.

The next day after the service, Bishop Hall asked me to join him and Bishop Felton Smith at a restaurant called Kathy Soul Food. It was about 15 minutes outside of Las Vegas in a city called Henderson, which I had never heard of. Instead of taking the freeway, he took his time and drove on the streets. I remember driving down a street called Russell. For some reason we made a left turned onto a street called Mountain Vista. I had a strange feeling that there was a church in the area, or that there should have been a church in that area.

When we arrived at the restaurant I asked Bishop Hall, "Are there any churches on this side of town?"

"No," he replied. "I have been trying for years to get someone to start a church out here. No one wants to do it because it is too far away.

The majority of churches affiliated with the Church of God in Christ were all west of downtown Las Vegas. That was about twelve to fifteen miles from the restaurant, if you took the freeway. Those miles are all in the city of Las Vegas. There were also no churches east of the restaurant in Henderson. Henderson had been rated the fastest growing city in America several times over the past five years.

After that conversation, I threw it out of my mind and went back to thinking about my own problems that were waiting for me back home in Sacramento.

When Edith and I returned to Sacramento, we received our business license and got right to work. A couple of days later, the Northern California Metropolitan Jurisdictional Workers and Leaders Conference was being held in Sacramento. Bishop Macklin called me and said, "Wynn, I need you to come down here with your wife and tell her to bring her computer and printer." He had no idea that we just started our business. On the last day of the conference the Bishop allowed one of the pastors to make an announcement encouraging the people to support our new business. We received so many clients from that one announcement that it brought us thousands of dollars of income. Many of them are clients that we still have to this day. Edith and I did a lot of work that week, not expecting any from the Bishop. We were just working like we have always done. At the end of the week, the Bishop gave us a very generous amount for our service at the conference.

Be Quick to Listen and Slow to Move

> *You are the average of the five people you spend the most time with*
>
> -Jim Rohn

As soon as we overcame a situation, it seemed like another attack on the church was just waiting around the corner. This one I did take personally. One day when I was in prayer, the Lord told me to warn the church about the spirit of lust. That Tuesday night, I taught on the subject of lust and fornication. What many of the people there did not realize was that they were allowing the god of lust to take over their consciousness. They listened to their gods, more than the Word of Almighty God. Because they did not take heed to the teaching, a month later eight people in the church were pregnant, youth and single adults. I was disappointed that they failed to take heed to the warning, but I kept encouraging them and loving them. I let them know that I was there even through this difficult time. They were like children to me and I instructed them just as I instructed my biological children.

One thing I praised God for was the fact that I always made time for my children. One of the many things I taught my children was how to face their problems. I told them, "If you run, eventually your problems will catch up with you. You do not have to learn the hard way." I talked to my children and let them know the dangers that were out there. I always reminded them that the choices they make always affect their future.

I did not just preach about choices to my family; I also tried to stay consistent with my church family. Since the incidents had happened, there was no sense in staying disappointed. This was the reality of it and being there for them meant more to me than turning away and leaving them to take this on by themselves. I tried very hard to help those young people and young adults who were pregnant learn how to be good parents according to the Bible. And because I was consistent with my love for them, they are still in church to this day.

God Never Said the Road Would Be Easy

> *History has demonstrated that the most notable winners usually encountered heartbreaking obstacles before they triumphed. They won because they refused to become discouraged by their defeats.*

-B.C. Forbes

We were near the end of our lease in the Sacramento location. I spoke with my brother-in-law, who worked at a high school in the school district. He said we could hold our weekly services in the theater of the school. I had a meeting with the members of church and they thought it was a great idea. So when the lease was up, we moved to the high school.

The lease for my home was also near an end. I had two months to decide where my family was going to live next. Edith and I prayed, consecrated ourselves and sought the Lord for weeks. I thought maybe my time was up for pastoring and that I should quit and become a good member of another church. It is not always an easy road following the Lord in difficult times, but that's when you need to hear from Him the most.

I was at home one day when my aunt called and said to me, "John, whatever the Lord has for you, it is for you. If the Lord has told you to move to Henderson, Nevada and start a church, you do it. I believe the Lord will go with you and bless you."

What my aunt did not know was that I had talked with Edith about moving to Henderson, Nevada, but was afraid to step out and move forward. That phone call confirmed what I had already felt in my spirit.

Chapter 7   Wrestling Lessons

You will encounter different situations in your life, but make sure you are not wrestling gods you created.

1. What gods have you created in your consciousness that you find yourself wrestling with continuously?

_____

_____

_____

_____

_____

2. Have you allowed these gods to control your mind? If so, how?

_____

_____

_____

_____

_____

3. Make a list of specific steps you need to take to eliminate these types of gods or thoughts from your consciousness.

_____

_____

_____

_____

_____

4. Why do you think it's important to follow the Word of God?

_____

_____

_____

_____

_____

Chapter 7   Wrestling Strategies

1. Five things to do when you are in a challenging situation:
    a. Identify the problem.
    b. Identify whether it is in your power to solve it.
    c. If it is in your power, then solve it.
    d. Identify the tools you need to solve it:
        •   Information.
        •   Counseling.
        •   Prayer.
        •   Faith.
        •   Reading Material, etc.
    e. If it is not in your power to solve it, identify someone with the expertise to assist you.

CHAPTER 8

DOWN, BUT NOT KNOCKED OUT

One night while I was asleep, I had dream in which I heard a group of people in Las Vegas saying "We are looking for a pastor." It was like the call for support that Paul received in the Book of Acts.

> *And a vision appeared to Paul in the night; There stood a man of Macedonia, and prayed him, saying, Come over into Macedonia, and help us.* (Acts 16:9)

I thought the dream was weird. When I woke up, I told Edith about it. For weeks I kept wondering why I had that dream. I prayed about it, and even though the Lord did not give me a specific answer, I began to feel the leading to start a church in the Henderson/Las Vegas area. I know what you are thinking, because I thought the same thing. I already had a church in Reno and another in Sacramento; I would have to be crazy to do something like that. I guess I'm crazy. I decided that I would pioneer a church in Las Vegas and have one service a week on Wednesday evenings only.

Edith and I flew to Las Vegas to find a building. I had no idea where I was going, so I asked my cousin to pick us up at the airport and drive me around. When we got off the plane, Edith said, "When we get there, you will know."

As soon as we left the airport, we drove around looking at different buildings. When we passed down Russell Road, something felt very familiar. I asked my cousin to turn down the next street, which happened to be Mountain Vista, the same street we were on when I went to dinner with Bishop Hall. I remembered having felt that it was a good area for a church.

After we turned onto Mountain Vista, I looked to my left and I said, "That's it! We don't have to look any further. I can go home now." There before us was a brand new building available for lease. We called the owner and negotiated a contract. It was an uncharted area for the Church of God in Christ in Las Vegas. In the sixty years of the jurisdictions, there was only one church that had set up ministry in that area, but it closed after only a short time. I knew the Lord would be with me in this venture. It was an amazing experience, because only one year had passed since my first visit to the area and my initial impression that a church was needed. Never in my wildest imagination, however, did I think I would be the pastor to launch a church there.

We returned to Sacramento, where I dove back into my silent wrestle with God, this time on the issue of a third church. I immediately started airing on cable television in Las Vegas announcing the church services. A few of the men from Sacramento drove with me to take chairs and equipment to set up the church, and we held our first service that same night. Visitors came that night because of the telecast; one lady even joined the church.

Later that night I asked the Lord, "What am I doing? Am I in your will?" I went to sleep and forgot all about what I asked God. Around four o'clock in the morning I woke up suddenly and heard the Lord speak to my spirit. He said, "I have given you an open door here in Las Vegas." I researched in the Bible and found that the open door meant great opportunities. I began to cry because I felt God had given me assurance that He was with me in starting the church in Las Vegas.

The next day I returned to Sacramento and shared my experiences with Edith. I told her what I had heard regarding the open door. Some of the thoughts and feelings I had when I was at the Las Vegas church were new to me. I could not adequately explain it to her because I did not understand it myself. I just knew I could not shake the feelings I was having.

She said, "Let's pray, and if the Lord is leading us to relocate our family to Henderson, we'll go."

I researched the City of Henderson on the internet, checking out everything from schools to grocery stores. I said to myself, "What are you doing? How can you pastor three churches and live in a brand new city? Are you crazy? You can't even handle the two churches you have."

On top of everything else, the biweekly drive to Reno started to get to me. I had been driving back and forth five hours round trip for two years, and it was becoming a chore. I had a growing feeling that I needed to do something different.

If you have ever traveled from Reno to Sacramento on Interstate 80, you know that the weather is not always the best during the winter months. It is a very stressful drive because of the mountains, the semi-trucks, and the unpredictable weather. However, every time it was time for me to go to Reno, the Lord opened the way. As I mentioned before, in the two years I commuted to Reno, I only had to put chains on the car once. That was a huge blessing.

As I weighed the pros and cons about our family moving to Las Vegas, the pros outweighed the cons, especially because of the fact that I would not have to drive to Reno anymore. I could easily fly between any of the three cities in just one hour.

Never Let Them See You Sweat

The man who complains about the way the ball bounces is likely the one who dropped it.

-Lou Holtz

At the time we started having worship services at the high school in Sacramento, I was still a little nervous about my decision to move to Henderson. Only a handful of people attended our first couple of services. Understandably, some people left the church because they were tired of moving. But even those who left the church will tell you to this day that everywhere the church moved, the power of God was there and people continued to be blessed. The Lord allowed us to understand early in ministry that it's not about a building. As long as the presence of the Lord was with us, we were going to be alright.

One Sunday when attendance was particularly small, I thought seriously about closing the church in Sacramento. I felt I had given my best in the city for several years and still only had a few people supporting the church. The following Sunday I told my Assistant Pastor, "It's time to shut the church down."

When we arrived for the service, however, the school was packed with people. "What is this?" I asked, amazed. Turning to my Assistant Pastor, I said, "Maybe we should wait a while on that decision to close." He replied, "Yes, I think so."

We never did close down the church.

The tests of both of these cities became very important to the growth of my ministry. I was a visionary who was not afraid to take on a project no matter how large or small. Being the pastor of the church in Reno taught me patience, focus and structure in business. Both churches stretched me spiritual and naturally; it was a test of strength, character and maturity.

I had two churches in two different cities, under two Bishops. The Church of God in Christ had different representatives in each state and in each jurisdiction of the state. My two churches were in two different jurisdictions, one in Nevada and one in California. I held leadership responsibilities in both jurisdictions. In California I was under the leadership of Bishop Jerry Macklin, who had sixty churches in his jurisdiction. I was the Chairman of the auxiliaries, which was comprised of the music, youth, evangelism, missions, and Sunday school ministry. In Nevada, I was under the leadership of Bishop Carruth Hall, who had thirty churches under his jurisdiction. I was a member of the Executive Board as well as the Chairman of the Trustee Board. I was the District Superintendent of the Northern Nevada District, which meant I was responsible for supervising five churches.

I had given my entire young life to the ministry and the church, yet I could not escape the feeling that something was out of balance. I kept trying to figure out what I was doing wrong. With all the moves we had made, with the church as well as with our family home, I felt like I was going around in circles and making no progress.

One day I remembered a message I preached when I was twenty-six years old titled, "Breaking the Cycle." I was tired but did not realize that I was in a silent wrestle with the "god" of instability. And yet, even in despite of my struggle, God said to me very clearly, "There is an open door for you in Henderson." That's when I became completely confident in the decision to move my family to Henderson. I had tried everything else; why not? Mike Murdock once said, "In order to get something you never had, you have to do something you've never done." I was about to discover how right he was.

Chapter 8   Wrestling Lessons

When you are faced with decisions, these are some questions you should ask yourself before you proceed.

1. How willing are you to make changes in your life in order to follow God? What losses are you prepared to take in making those changes (people, places, things, etc.)?

    _____

    _____

    _____

    _____

    _____

2. Ask yourself this question: "Am I in the will of Almighty God?" How do you know?

    _____

    _____

    _____

    _____

3. When is moving in a new direction in your life worth fighting for? What criteria do you use in choosing your battles?

    _____

    _____

    _____

    _____

4. Write down a few decisions you could make that you know would be great for you but not for others. Which would you choose, and why?

    _____

    _____

    _____

    _____

Chapter 8   Wrestling Strategies

1. Count up the cost before making major moves.
    *   Profit and Loss (Finances).
    *   Timeframe (Dates and time of year).
    *   Pros and cons (The good, the bad, and the ugly).
    *   The emotional, physical, mental and spiritual effect (Family, friends, foes).

2. Things to remember when making decisions.
    *   In all thy ways acknowledge Almighty God.
    *   Pray, fast and read the Bible.
    *   Study the things you desire.
    *   Be willing to take full responsibility for your decision.
    *   Don't be afraid.
    *   Enjoy yourself.
    *   Don't look back.

LOCATION
OF THE MATCH

Facts do not cease to exist because they are ignored.
-Aldous Huxley

On July 23, 2002, my family along with my mother-in-law, loaded the cars and moved to Las Vegas. It was an unsettling feeling not knowing what our future held. All we knew was that we were moving to a new level in our lives. The enemy tried to attack us with the spirit of fear. It was a bit scary, but the word of God was louder than our fear. I kept hearing, "Perfect love casts *out all fear"* (1 John 4:18b) and "The blessing of the Lord, it maketh rich, and *adds no sorrow* with it" *(*Proverbs 10:22) The house we were trying to buy was not ready for us to move into, so a family friend who worked for a resort hotel made us a reservation with her time-share at her employee rate for two weeks. When we arrived in Las Vegas, the time-share hotel suite was not available until the next night, so on my family's first night in Las Vegas, we stayed at the church building we had already leased. Edith and her mother went to Wal-Mart and purchased pillows, sheets and blankets. What else could we do? All the hotels were full due to a convention that was in town.

Two weeks after our arrival in Las Vegas, our real estate agent told us that the owner of the home we were going to purchase had pulled out of the deal and opened escrow with someone else. As if that were not bad enough, we lost thousands of dollars that we had put down on the house, and could not get our money back. My first thought was to go back to Sacramento because we did not have a place to stay. I had enough money for the two-week hotel reservation, but only $250.00 to feed my family. We felt like we were living in a nightmare.

No Pain, No Gain

I remember the day I spent my last dollar for food. I did not have any more money and I did not know how I was going to feed my children. In despair, I called out to God, "Lord, you told me it was an open door." I began to cry. After driving around by myself for several hours talking to God, I drove to the church.

While I was there, one of my sisters called. She said, "God told me to send you $400.00 dollars."

When you are a man of faith, God allows you to press past the limits of your comfort zone. He does this so you will learn to trust Him no matter how dark your circumstances look. The Lord will let you know that you can depend on Him to touch someone's heart to bless you.

We were allowed to stay in the resort hotel for two additional weeks and the Lord provided the finances we needed. But again, I was still struggling with the same problem I dealt with in Sacramento; I had to find a house. Along with trying to settle my family, I was still trying to figure out how I was going to travel back and forth between three churches. Another important reason we had moved to Las Vegas was because I got tired of driving back and forth to my churches, and Las Vegas had an international airport that would allow me to fly back and forth.

One day the Holy Spirit said, "Let each church pay one way when you travel and it will not put a strain on any one church." I immediately implemented that plan, it worked wonderfully for years. I started having services in Las Vegas on Sunday morning at 8:00am in order to have time to fly to the other two cities and make it in time for services. The early morning service also allowed me to attend the other churches more frequently. When we began in Las Vegas, only my own family was in attendance.

This was tough for me because I had already experienced this years before, and here I was, starting all over again. Standing up to preach and seeing only my wife and children sitting there was mentally challenging to me. I could easily have become very discouraged, but I thought to myself, "Well, if this is what God wants me to do, train, teach and preach to my own family, I will do it. I will build them up for the future."

So often, we as pastors leave our children in the background because we want to protect them. Unfortunately, in our efforts to protect them, we are likely to lose them in ministry. I did not realize how much talent my children had because I was too busy developing the talents of my members instead of my children.

> *Train up a child in the way he should go: and when he*
> *is old, he will not depart from it.* (Proverbs 22:6)

When we first opened the church in Las Vegas, I was playing the keyboard, singing praise and worship, and then preaching the Word of God. It did not take long for that to get old. So one day I asked my 8-year-old daughter Farrah to take the microphone and sing for me. When we finally got a set of drums for the church, my son Jeremiah began playing them. He had always loved the drums, but he had not had very much practice. The more he played, the better he got. In Sacramento, I never realized the gifts in my own children because I never gave them a chance. I was too busy saving a building and depending on my sisters to sing. I had professional musicians, so my sons, who were very talented, got lost in the shuffle. Their gifts lay dormant until we moved to Las Vegas, and it was there that the Lord made room for them.

Willing to Pay the Price

> *I learned that the only way you are going to get anywhere*
> *in life is to work hard at it. Whether you're a musician,*
> *a writer, an athlete, or a businessman, there is no getting*
> *around it. If you do, you'll win- if you don't you won't.*
> -Bruce Jenner

For two weeks we were unsuccessful in finding a home. We were down to the wire with two days left in the hotel when Edith found a place to rent. But when the landlord saw on the application how many children we had, she changed her mind. She said she did not want that many people in her home. Edith cried as she sat down at the kitchen table in the resort. She said, "I never thought I would be denied a place to live because of having too many children."

The sound of Edith's crying tore at my heart, and I had to go to God for myself. It was Friday and we had to move out of the resort on Saturday. The managers of the resort had extended our reservation as long as they could. Someone else was checking in to our suite the next afternoon.

Living at risk is jumping off the cliff and building your wings on the way down.

-Ray Bradbury

As the head of my household, I went into the bedroom, closed the door behind me, and began to pray. I began my prayer as I normally did, asking God to give me a place for my family. This time, God spoke to me right away and said, "Don't ask me for anything; just praise me." For two hours straight I praised God in that hotel room. My back was up against the wall and it was a difficult place to be, but the Lord told me to praise him, and that's what I did. When I finished praying, I assured Edith that everything was going to be alright.

I bought a newspaper, looked in the classifieds for the Henderson area and saw a listing for a house that from the description sounded very nice. I called the number and spoke with a man who had a commanding and powerful voice. He began to share with me the vital information about the house: square footage, floor plan, number of bedrooms, etc. Then he said, "Just come see the house. We will talk about the payments and deposit when you get there."

When we arrived at the home, it was indeed very nice. We were impressed with the floor plan and the large bedrooms for my children. The owner said, "If you like it, you can have it." We did not fill out an application and he did not run a credit or a background check. He simply said, "The rent is $2200.00 per month, but I will prorate this month and go ahead and make payments on the deposit. Just give me $500.00 and you can move in tomorrow."

This was the blessing I was looking for. God continued showing me He was with us. We moved into the house with no furniture because all of our furniture was in storage in Sacramento. At that moment, we did not mind. After thirty days of living in a hotel, we were just glad to have a home.

The day we moved into the house, friends of ours invited us to dinner and welcomed us to the city. By the time we left their home, they had given us beds, blankets, televisions, a dining room table and chairs, and just about everything else we needed. They were so kind to us. We thanked God for touching their hearts and asking us to come over for dinner. It is a blessing when you are going through tough times and God sends people to aid you in your time of struggle. We developed a deeper understanding of God's promise from Isaiah:

> *When thou pass through the waters, I will be with thee; and through the rivers, they shall not overflow thee: when thou walkest through the fire, thou shalt not be burned; neither shall the flame kindle upon thee. (Isaiah 43:2)*

The Lord kept proving His word to me by blessing us from the day we arrived in the city of Las Vegas. When we felt we were at the end of our rope, God always manifested His Word to me. It did not matter how severe the test was or the trial of my faith, I knew that God was teaching me to depend on Him and not on man. God was going to get all the glory!

New Levels

God always gave me the strength to bounce back and go forward after I faced difficult situations. I just wished the situations were fewer and farther in between! When I wrote my first book *New Levels, New Devils* in 2002, I wrote about how the devil attacks people through different media such as television, the internet, books, and video games. I stated how at each new level, we attain new D.E.V.I.L.S.: Deceptions, Enemies, Victims, Issues, Lies and Struggles that challenge our future. I expressed how at every level you reach, the enemy waits to attack you in order to take you out. He tries to prevent you from reaching your goals, dreams and levels in God.

Before my book release I wanted to make my mentor received the first copy. I will never forget the day I met with him. After I handed him a copy of the book, he released me from being the AIM Chairman (Auxiliaries in Ministry). I was surprised and hurt, more so because I had been so excited about giving him the book and expected to walk away feeling good. Instead, I left feeling sad and disappointed. I understood in my mind even then that he had done this because he felt I had too much on my plate, but it hurt just the same. Later on, I came to really appreciate what he did, because it blessed me in the long run.

I returned home to Las Vegas on January 29, 2003, it was my 31st birthday. Edith and the kids took me to dinner at the restaurant on the 103rd floor of the Stratosphere Hotel. They kept the location a surprise, so I had no idea where we were going to until we got there. When we stepped off the elevator and walked into a beautiful banquet room on the top floor of the hotel, a large group of people yelled, "Surprise!!" Many of my friends were there and I was indeed surprised. Edith had planned a combination surprise birthday party and release celebration for my book, *New Levels, New Devils*. It was wonderful and helped me forget about my disappointment of a few days earlier. The following month we released the book at a celebration in Sacramento.

Scheduling Conflict

In Sacramento, I was still facing challenges in finding a permanent location for my church. After six months, we moved our services from the high school to The Heritage Hotel. They had a very nice theater that they allowed us to lease. In order for me to fly in and attend the services on time, I changed the Sacramento Sunday worship time to 2:30pm. This was a sure test of the membership's faith in the vision while continuing to follow me even though I was no longer living in Sacramento. Thankfully, I had a good leadership team who stood by me and continued doing the work. I continued this schedule for an entire year.

Not surprisingly, however, these arrangements caused conflicts in the congregation. Even as I pursued the vision, I had to deal with people who were causing division in the church. Some of the members murmured and complained about the schedule because they wanted to start the service at 11:00am instead of 2:30pm. Others were pleased at the fact that I made an effort to attend the services as often as I did.

After a while, some of the people who had been members for years began to leave the church because they could not conceive the vision of one church in multiple locations. Their vision was for me to be in the city to preach directly to them every time the doors were open. Eventually, I changed the time back to 11:00am, but that did not stop the murmuring.

For where two or three are gathered together in my name, there am I in the midst of them. (Matthew 18:30)

It was complicated leading people who did not want to follow the vision. I drew my strength from the Lord, but also from my wife and children, who have always supported me in all of my efforts. The odd thing is that I found myself being questioned by my own family members; cousins and sisters who could not see my vision. Having three churches in three different cities was new to the West Coast and people did not know how to handle it. My extended family did not have faith in me at the time because they had no idea how this could possibly work. One family member actually invited some of the faithful members of our church to switch to another family member's church in another city.

I always stressed to the leaders in the church that Sunday mornings are special times to serve the people in the community. If they want to visit another church, they should do so during the week or on Sunday evenings; I didn't mind. What bothered me was to arrive on Sunday morning and discover that half the church was empty. People would visit other churches without letting anybody in the leadership know where they were. This always hurt deeply when I found out about it later.

> *Resentment is like drinking poison and then hoping it will kill your enemies.*
>
> -Nelson Mandela

I never thought my own flesh and blood would treat me as though I were a task master overworking people to the point where she felt that she needed to set them free. Maybe she thought of herself as the "Harriett Tubman" of my church, trying to free the people through her own underground railroad. She made our church sound like it was a prison. Some members claimed that they could no longer get a breakthrough at our church and had decided to go to my other sister's church.

The manner in which all this was being done made me so angry that I wrote a letter to every member in all three of the churches. It was a passionate letter in which I explained the mandate I had on my life and what God had called me to do in all of the ministries. I thought that with this letter, which I titled, "From the Heart of the Pastor," things might change.

They did; they got worse. Key people in leadership positions left our church and joined my other family member's church in another city. The pastor of that other church was never involved in any of this and I never blamed him. What I found hardest to believe was that my own sister would lead these people away from me because she couldn't understand what God was doing in my life.

I will never forget how fast the membership dropped. While we were losing members in Sacramento at an astonishing rate, the members in Reno were still calling me a "part time pastor" because I couldn't attend all of the weekly services. Members there are also began to leave and join other churches. Some of the saints who left the church in Reno had been members for more than 20 years, ever since my father was the pastor.

I cried, prayed and asked God what to do. He told me to stay the course, so I did. As people were leaving the churches in Sacramento and

Reno, the Lord was giving us increase in Las Vegas. Many ask, "Why didn't you just focus on Las Vegas?" I wish I could tell them. All I knew was that this was the assignment God had given me. I knew I had to be faithful to Him and to His work until He released me. My absolute conviction that God had called me to this gave me confidence.

Be Faithful Until Death

> *A successful person realizes his personal responsibility for self-motivation. He starts with himself because he possesses the key to his own ignition switch.*
>
> -Kemmons Wilson

When you are a leader you cannot change the course because people provoke you or leave the church. If you change direction because of the people; God cannot depend on you to do His will. That is how Moses got in trouble with God. He allowed the people to cause him to do something other than what God instructed him to do. God told him to speak to the rock. But because the people frustrated him, he hit the rock and called them rebels. Because of his disobedience, God did not allow Moses to enter the Promised Land.

I made up my mind that I wanted all that God had for me. In the process of doing His work, the Lord began to bless the church in Las Vegas and send in people, but that still did not seem like enough for me. I could not enjoy the blessings because I was focused on the failures. I longed for a response from God to my unanswered questions. I kept trying to figure out why the Lord was blessing the church in Las Vegas so early in its ministry. Everything I tried to do in Sacramento did not work, but I come to Vegas and it does work? Go figure.

Forgive and Move On

> *As long as you don't forgive, who and whatever it is will occupy rent –free space in your mind.*
>
> -Isabelle Holland

117

What was this all about? Even though the church was blessed and people were joining, I felt like something was wrong with me. Maybe I was the cause of the other two churches not prospering.

I was preparing myself and developing an insight on leadership that I had not experienced before. I began to understand my call at a greater level. In the midst of all the transitions with the churches, I had to find a place in God that was giving me strength to focus. Yet I still had this wrestle inside of me that I could not put my finger on.

When I moved to Las Vegas, I was so broken that I had lost confidence in my ministry and myself. I was ashamed and felt like a failure because of the situations the churches in Sacramento and Reno were in. I tried to do everything I could in those cities and wondered why God did not manifest himself. I was disappointed in myself and emotionally damaged.

There is a pastor in Las Vegas who is an old friend of my family. When we moved there I had breakfast with him every morning for weeks. He had no idea what I was going through, but God gave him exactly what to say to me every day. One time he said, "God has given you such a great anointing; don't let the devil minimize your gift." Another time he told me, "You are one of the greatest of preachers, and God uses you mightily." He literally counseled me and built me back up. It wasn't flattery; it was empowerment. He helped me regain my focus and realize that I was still deeply hurt.

In chapter two I asked God why He didn't allow me to purchase the building on 65th Street. It took three years before He answered me. One day I was watching an old videotape of a message I had preached on 65th Street. As I watched the video, I asked God again, "Why?"

Finally, He answered me and said, "I will never give you something that you want more than Me."

I started weeping, and the first phase of my healing began. It took me three years to start recovering from the hurt and pain of the loss I experienced in Sacramento. I did not realize I had made this facility another idol god in my consciousness. Unknowingly, I had made that building on 65th Street a point of reference as to whether or not God was with me. God reminded me that He was always with me, with or without a building.

My healing had begun; however, I was still wrestling with God in my faith and belief. I gradually came to understand that God did not want me to be comfortable in the city of Sacramento because otherwise I would not have launched out into the deep. God has a mandate on our lives. He is in control. The Lord showed me that I would experience loss, feel hurt, get angry, and watch people turn their back on me. But He told me that it did not matter what other people did, because only what I did for Christ was going to last.

I believe very strongly in following leadership. All through my life I have been fortunate to have great leaders setting examples for me. Every now and then I would implement some of the training I had received from my leaders, and when I did, it always worked. Much of the success I have enjoyed in many aspects of ministry is due simply to following the example of the leaders who mentored me. They were also an invaluable source of wisdom and information for me.

One thing I never asked from any of my leaders or mentors, however, was financial support either for my family or for any of the three churches. The Lord has always provided for us in that regard, and I am grateful. I am a man of faith who has trusted in the Lord all of my life. In everything I do, I seek to give God all of the glory.

After I started the third church, other pastors from various denominations approached me asking lots of questions. I had several Bishops, Superintendents, leaders of our national church and other pastors ask me, "How do you do what you do?" Out of respect for them I gave them some of my time and explained the plan that God had given me. In turn, they told me what *they* thought I should do. The pressure of fielding so many questions from so many different people became so great that it was driving me crazy.

I received more advice as the pastor of three churches than I ever did when I only had one. The funny thing is that none of those who were advising me had three churches. They either had one church or no church at all. I always try to listen politely and be open-minded, because you never know when or from whom an important word from God or invaluable insight might come. However, I knew in my heart that I had to follow God's instruction for my life, regardless of what anybody else said. Many times I wanted to listen to other people's ideas, but I knew from whence my help cometh; my help cometh from the Lord. He was the one who gave me the strength to work in ministry in the first place.

Other than Edith, my wife, God was the only one I could turn to late in the midnight hour. I knew that if I wanted to continue receiving direction from Him, I would have to be obedient when He spoke to me. Even though I wasn't always popular in my decisions, God always brought me through. Just when it seemed as though all the odds were against me, the Lord would work a miracle and everyone would give Him the glory.

Chapter 9   Wrestling Lessons

When you are going through transition, here are some thoughts and questions you need to consider.

1. Never allow others to control your thoughts through anger, resentment and hurt. Forgive and move on. Describe a time in your life when you allowed someone to control you because of anger, pain, or pleasure. What were the results?

_____

_____

_____

_____

_____

2. When you are going through a process that you do not understand, learn to be quiet and pray until you receive clarity. Are you speaking before it is time?

_____

_____

_____

_____

_____

3. Write down the names of people who have offended you. Ask God to help you forgive them both in your mind and soul so that you can live, grow, and prosper.

_____

_____

_____

_____

_____

Chapter 9   Wrestling Strategies

1. Family and friends are human; they can be influenced by others as well.
   - Write their names down, pray for them, forgive them, and release them.

2. If you are going to be successful in life, keep a positive spirit and do not allow bitterness to motivate you to succeed.

3. Enjoy your success and blessings with a pure heart. You will live a longer and happier life without bittersweet feelings.

CHAPTER 10

A MIND
WRESTLE

Humble yourselves therefore under the mighty hand of
God, that he may exalt you in due time: Casting all your
care upon him; for he careth for you. (1 Peter 5:6-7)

The Mindset in Sacramento

One day I received a call from the hotel in Sacramento where we were having church. They informed me that they had been bought out by another company and that we had to move out. "Here we go again!" I thought. I was fed up with moving from place to place but had no choice because we did not have the revenue we needed to purchase anything. We had enough money saved to pay the first and last month's rent, so I looked for another building to lease. As I began to reflect on all of the moves we had made, the enemy began to play mind games with me. My mind was so troubled with the many disappointing memories of the past concerning the Sacramento church location that I was apprehensive about its future existence. I began to question whether or not it would continue.

This manuscript of yours that has just come back from
another editor is a precious package. Don't consider it rejected.
Consider that you've addressed it "to the editor who can ap-

preciate my work" and it has simply come back stamped "not at this address." Just keep looking for the right address.

-Barbara Kingsolver

The Mindset in Reno

The Lord began to bless our district in Reno. It was great news because other pastors started to join us and I was encouraged. When you have been in ministry battles, you become especially grateful for the blessings you receive. I've never done drugs, smoked, drank or been unfaithful to my wife. However, at times, I believe that working in ministry can be just as much of a struggle, because when you have come out of troubled situations and your circumstances do not change for the better, old habits of doubt or fear can drive you back into a defeated mindset.

For we wrestle not against flesh and blood, but against principalities, against powers, against the rulers of the darkness of this world, against spiritual wickedness in high places. (Ephesians 6:12)

The Mindset in Las Vegas

In Las Vegas we had a radio program. One day I was preaching and it was going well, drawing in listeners from all walks of life. My heart and mind, however, were still in Sacramento. I suppose my thoughts and prayers were so consumed by that church because it was my first church. I had given everything I had to see the people go to another level. My mind was playing tricks on me because, even though I was glad about the blessings and the growth in Las Vegas, the people did not have my spirit. I felt like I had birthed the church in Sacramento and that I was their spiritual father. When parents conceive and give birth to a child, that child has characteristics of both the mother and the father. When I started the church in Las Vegas, it seemed that many people came to our church to escape something else. I did not feel like they were coming to be developed by our ministry as much as to run from a ministry that may have let them down or caused them great pain.

I welcomed them, of course, and was glad they were there, but they did not look like me or act like any of the children to whom I had given spiritual birth to. They were more like patients in a hospital in need of a physician. I felt led by the Spirit to bring healing to their broken hearts and to care for them for a season.

In Sacramento, I had spiritual children whom I had birthed in prayer. I spent a lot of time with them; they began to act like me and pick up some of my spiritual characteristics. Some of the women began to act, dress and even pray like my wife. Of course, I did not realize this until we relocated to Las Vegas.

Even though you have ten thousand guardians in Christ, you do not have many fathers, for in Christ Jesus I became your father through the gospel. (1 Corinthians 4:15)

I knew that God was going to bless the church to do what I saw in my spirit, but I also needed this at the time that they were not ready. I remember one Bible study night at the Las Vegas church when only five people attended. That night I talked about my vision of the church, the vision that I believed the Lord had assigned to me to in spite of my location. I always tried to stay true to the vision at all costs.

Part of my vision and my desire was to start a childcare center, job training, and a GED program. That night there was a returning visitor who had not yet decided whether or not to become a part of the ministry. I made a comment about John F. Kennedy's statement during the Bay of Pigs controversy: "Ask not what your country can do for you; ask what you can do for your country." Then I paraphrased it, saying, "Don't ask what the church can do for you, but ask what you can do for the church."

You've got to ask! Asking is, in my opinion, the world's most powerful and neglected secret to success and happiness.
-Percy Ross

Because of that one statement, this visitor came up to me after the service and said, "I heard your vision and I know someone who can get you started with the childcare and community development center."

I couldn't believe it! I had been trying to start a childcare center and job training for years in Sacramento but could never get it off of the ground. Now, in Las Vegas and with only five people in the service, I had shared my vision and this woman grabbed hold of it. She also was instrumental in helping my wife and me with the overall vision of the community development center. I am still reaping the harvest from the information and assistance that one woman gave me seven years ago. Even though there were only five people in the service, the Lord used one woman whose belief in my ministry led to information that changed the church.

Back in Sac Town

After a good bit of searching, I finally found another building in the Oak Park area of Sacramento. I negotiated a reasonable price for the 4000 square-foot building, but the owner did not want me to sign on it alone. So for the very first time in our ministry, I asked two of the men in the church to sign with me. Without hesitation they both said yes. I had never wanted anyone to sign on a lease for the church because I did not want them to feel responsible if the church was not able to maintain it.

We had a meeting with the church and I showed them the building. Together we examined the possibilities of the building and discussed how we could lease it for three to five years. When everyone was in agreement, we signed the lease and went to work again. The members had a mind to work and the church was doing well. This was such a relief to see that it sparked optimism in my spirit again. I was reminded once again that God was faithful and would bring us through.

When it was time to set up my team, I asked one of my sisters to assist me, offering to give her a love gift if she would speak for me once a month. I literally begged her to help, but she said, "No!"

At that time in her life she was traveling a lot and could not commit because of her hectic schedule. Even though the situations in her life were uncontrollable, and despite all the good things God was doing, I still allowed the "god" of negativity to take precedence in my mind. I simply could not get myself together on this one. What started as a personal issue for me became a spiritual issue. I felt that since I had been there for her, she should be there for me. As a result of my inconsiderate behavior stemming from my pain, we barely spoke to each other for two years.

In spite of this wrestle, the church in Sacramento was growing. The church in Reno actually started growing too. A former pastor who closed his church came and joined our congregation along with his former members. I was excited to see that our churches were finally taking a turn for the better. Both churches were encouraged, and my spirit took a much-needed boost. I was seeing movement now, yet I still had issues inside me that I was trying to deal with. The blessing of the Lord does not always stop because you have issues. This is why you must always rehearse your purpose and do a spiritual checkup on your life. Some of us can get away with having issues and remain successful in the natural eyes of men, but God is always weighing our hearts.

After being gone for three years, my sister decided to come back to the Sacramento church in May of 2007. We started talking to each other again and she began working with us in the ministry. I still did not trust her, however, because I felt she had crossed me and I did not want to be hurt again.

One day she called me to talk about the church. She told me what she thought we needed to do and what things needed to be changed. During the conversation the pain inside me welled up all over again. It was the same hurt as when we were in the building on 65th Street, when I felt like I wasn't being accepted by either God or the people. I became so angry that I hung up on her and immediately called another one of my sisters. I began screaming at the top of my voice about how angry and hurt I was at the sister I had just hung up on, and how she was starting to tear down the church again. Between the crying and the screaming, I had almost lost control. My anger threatened to overwhelm me.

My sister on the phone tried to calm me down. "It's all right, John," she said. "Everything will be all right. Try not to worry about what was said.

All blame is a waste of time. No matter how much fault you find with another, and regardless of how much you blame him, it will not change you.

-Wayne Dyer

The next day I had to minster at a church in Reno for a men's conference. I was still very hurt and I really did not want to go. "How can I preach when I'm feeling like this?" I asked myself. Nevertheless, I got on the plane and flew to Reno. It was a Saturday morning and the subject of my message was, "What it means to be a servant." In the middle of my message, I began to cry. I was preaching and crying and could not stop. Once again, my mind was playing tricks on me.

Many of the men, who heard my message, including a number of bishops, were moved to tears by the impact of my words. The Lord used me to minister healing to men who were broken, but what they did not know was that I was wrestling with hurt and disappointment myself. It was no longer a silent wrestle; now it became a personal wrestle between me and God.

After I finished speaking, I went into the office and sat down. As I continued to cry, the Lord spoke to me and said, "It's not your sister, the churches, or the finances that you have been angry about. You have been fighting with little gods in your subconscious mind for 10 years."

What is Wrestling?

The definitions of wrestling are: "to engage in a wrestle, to contend with in a wrestle as in a struggle for mastery; grapple; to force by or as if by wrestling."

As I look over these situations, I see similarities from Esau and Jacob in the wrestle that Jacob had with his brother. Let me explain the wrestles that both Jacob and I experienced in our lives. In the Hebrew language, the name "Israel" means "struggling with God." This is the name Jacob was given after he wrestled with "the angel of the Lord," or God. Jacob was afraid to face his brother Esau because of the tricks Jacob had played on him in order to steal Esau's birthright as well as the fatherly blessing from Isaac that was rightfully his as the firstborn. Jacob's deception made Esau so angry that he wanted to kill Jacob.

Now, years later, Jacob knew that he was going to meet up with his brother Esau; he went to a place by himself to consult Almighty God about this meeting. He wanted God to save him from his brother. Jacob began to wrestle within himself and said to the angel, "I'm not going to let you go until you bless me." Because of Jacob's persistence in the wrestling match, the angel said, "I'm going to bless you. However, I'm first going to change your name from Jacob, which means 'supplanter' or 'trickster,' to 'Israel,' meaning, 'one who has wrestled with God.'"

What I have discovered is that my wrestle was not the same as Jacob's. As time went on, I discovered that I had Almighty God on my side; that He was with me and blessing me. But I had formed a god in my subconscious mind that I allowed to take my focus off of the true and living God. God said to me, "You are not wrestling with me; you are wrestling with your own little gods, which are the gods of fear, worry, uncertainty, financial instability and, most of all, doubt."

When God showed me that my true wrestle was in my own mind, I began to weep and scream. I asked Him to forgive me for allowing my mind to get in the way of my worship, praise, success, and faith in Him.

Many people today have the same trials and don't even know it. They wrestle with the same kinds of false gods that had captured my mind but are completely unaware of it. We all face potential wrestling matches every day simply because of the trials and tribulations we experience from time to time. In the midst of our troubles it's easy to forget that the Bible teaches that God allows trials because they make us strong. If we didn't have any trials, we would not be able to tell someone how we made it through.

Once God revealed this to me, my wrestle began to stop and so did my quest for greatness in people, places and things. Once I let go of the little gods in my subconscious mind and focused on the will of Almighty God, my life started to change. Healing took place, restoration came to my life, and resources opened up to me. My life began to make sense. I now understood my journey.

What I have shared with so many people is that real truth cannot be studied; it must be revealed by God Himself. It wasn't until Saul was on his way to kill the saints at Jerusalem that he fell to the earth and a great light appeared from heaven unto him and said, "Saul, Saul, why persecutest thou me?"

> *And he fell to the earth, and heard a voice saying unto him, Saul, Saul, why persecutest thou me? And he said, Who art thou, Lord? And the Lord said I am Jesus whom thou persecutest: it is hard for thee to kick against the pricks. And he trembling and astonished said, Lord, what wilt thou have me to do? And the Lord said unto him, Arise, and go into the city, and it shall be told thee what thou must do.* (Acts 9:4-6)

When God reveals Himself to you, your search for truth ends and your wrestle for acceptance ceases because you now understand who Almighty God is vs. who the little "gods" are in your life.

Chapter 10 Wrestling Lessons

It's very important to protect your mind when you are engaged in spiritual and natural battles.

1. Your mind is the gateway to dreams, visions, pain and pleasure. What is moving you in your mind today: pain or pleasure? Why?

_____

_____

_____

_____

_____

2. Whatever thoughts you allow to occupy your mind will control you. What thoughts are you allowing to control you? Are these the thoughts that should control you? If not, what steps will you take to change those thoughts?

_____

_____

_____

_____

_____

3. If you are not mentally prepared for success, it does not matter what you have; you will not be satisfied.
    Define what success means to you. Then compare your definition of success with the Bible's definition. The Book of Proverbs is a good place to start.

_____

_____

_____

_____

_____

Chapter 10 Wrestling Strategies

1. Focus on things you can control.
    - Prayer.
    - Praise.
    - Positive thinking.

2. Get rid of the "Stinking Thinking".
    - Doubt.
    - Fear.
    - Worry.
    - Insecurity.

3. 20% of success is mechanical and 80% is internal.

4. Change "you" and everything else will change.

5. Focus on what does not irritate you.

6. Your strongest thoughts move you towards your purpose.

CHAPTER 11

WEARY WRESTLER

My prayer life was more real now than ever before. The time I spent with God was from my heart and the ministry of praying for other people took on a new sense of urgency and joy. Most of all, I was serious about my duties and responsibilities. However, my perspective of what I thought God should do was wrong. For a long time I never realized that I had looked for God's manifestation in the physical and natural trappings of church buildings and facilities more than I had the things He did in the hearts of His people. I was a young man in ministry with no information on how to focus on the unseen. I just knew that the Bible said to walk by faith and not by sight. When I look back now, one of the things I wish I had done was to simply enjoy my journey. Edith has always said to me, "You should enjoy your life today; these may be the best days of our lives."

Not that I didn't have a good time working in ministry. I was just under so much pressure as a young pastor that at times it seemed like the bad outweighed the good. The most exciting time in ministry for me is when I see the smile on a person's face after he or she has been healed, delivered or set free from difficult circumstances.

Next to that, I must say that working in the Church of God in Christ in the jurisdictions as well as on the national level has afforded me some pretty exciting experiences. All my life I have enjoyed being around the saints, so if I can work to make the program smoother or play a small part in assisting my leader, I feel good. I praise God for the skills, talents and abilities He has given me and I enjoy contributing to the overall success of an event. I love being the type of person who tries to make sure everyone is feeling alright. I like to make people smile. That is just a part of my character.

> *The individual who wants to reach the top in business must appreciate the might and force of habit. He must be quick to break those habits that can break him - and hasten to adopt those practices that will become the habits that help him achieve the success he desires.*
>
> -J. Paul Getty

I have endured many challenges in the positions I have served, from District Superintendent to Jurisdictional Youth President. From a young man's perspective, I was so grateful for the opportunity to work and serve; I never gave any thought to the obstacles I might encounter. I had a "Bring it on!" mentality. I was determined to work with everything I had, just to see the smiles on the faces of the saints who enjoyed themselves praising the Lord. That was reward enough; I was willing to work for free because ministry was my life and I enjoyed serving God's people.

If you can believe it, as I began working in higher levels of ministry, I sometimes was criticized for smiling too much! People would get upset when they saw me coming. They said I was, "too jolly." No, I was free! I believe that he whom the Son sets free is free indeed. I didn't have to walk around bound by circumstances.

In the midst of everything I had experienced in my life, I never looked like I had the world on my shoulders. You couldn't tell I was going through anything. I would travel to meetings all over the country, excited about working with my leaders. I simply had to push a mental pause button on what I was wrestling with until I returned home. I knew my objective was to help lighten the load of my leaders; I couldn't focus on my wrestle with the churches at the same time. So before I left home, I was determined to enjoy my trip and make my contribution to the workload that was waiting for me. When I got off of an airplane in a city, I got off with a smile on my face, excited and ready to get to work.

During my tenure as the Jurisdictional Youth President in Nor Cal Metropolitan, I was afforded a great opportunity to become the very first youth president in a new jurisdiction. Bishop Macklin allowed me to be creative and to set up the youth department from the ground up, and I was honored. I learned so much from working under such a visionary leader; he inspired me to shoot for the moon. Les Brown said, "If you shoot for the moon and you miss, you will at least land among the stars." I was determined to make the department a success and enjoyable for all of the youth and children. I created a handbook for all youth leaders and workers in the local church, in the district, and in the jurisdiction. I worked diligently in the department, striving for excellence because of the example I had before me in my jurisdictional Bishop.

For all that I contributed to the jurisdiction's youth department, what I learned was even greater. I had the opportunity to gain detailed knowledge about different aspects of the jurisdiction and the national denominational organization. From a variety of leaders I learned a great deal about jurisdictional protocol and behavior. These leaders were experienced survivors who had endured the terrain of this type of ministry for years. Working in ministry at this level requires a lot of patience and faith in God. I learned how to stay focused, even when others tried to discredit my ideas and abilities.

Sometimes, when you are climbing the mountains of success at different levels in the church, you find yourself alone. My loneliness pushed me closer into the arms of the Lord Jesus Christ. I found my strength in praying and reading the Bible. These spiritual disciplines encouraged me not to be bitter when faced with adversity.

God has always spoken to me through His Word. One day I was challenged by a leader who did some evil things to me that left me greatly bothered in my spirit. I was frustrated but wanted to be sure I was making the right decision. I went to the church to pray and the Lord spoke to me and said, "The steps of a good man are ordered by the Lord." Continuing, He said, "You will never know what type of man you are until you are in the presence of wickedness." He concluded with, "In all your ways acknowledge Me, and I will direct your path." He filled me with His loving assurance that I was not alone and that He would lead me in the direction that was best for me.

Taking Control of the Wrestle

In the summer of 2007 I became impatient with waiting for things to go my way after so many years of trying to please other people. I said to myself, "I've had it!" The financial problems of the church in Sacramento reappeared and it had eaten at me long enough. I was unhappy with the positions I held in both jurisdictions because I had allowed people to frustrate my purpose. I decided that it was time for John Wynn to do what John Wynn wanted to do. With that determination, I enrolled in the University of Nevada Las Vegas as a fulltime student to finish my degree in sociology.

I told myself that it was fine if members of the churches didn't want to work for a better tomorrow, but I was determined to work for a better future for my wife and my family." I let all of the churches know that I wasn't going to be attending any of the weekly services for a while because I was going back to school. I gave every church a preaching schedule for Bible study and told them I would see them on the Sundays when I was scheduled to preach. I finally could use some of the same excuses I had heard for years: "I can't come to church because I have to go to school," or, "I have homework tonight."

I was tired and fed up with all the politics in the different offices in the local church as well as in the jurisdictions. Frankly, I was just plain frustrated with my journey. So I began to do things my way. I said to myself, "If I have to move, fine. If I have to change locations, so be it. If I have to quit my positions, fine. Whatever I have to do to better myself and my family in ministry, I am going to do just that." Our childcare center was blessed and bringing in the revenue we needed to support the work in the church and community in Las Vegas. Our retail clothing store also was doing well.

In September, for our 13th year Appreciation, all three churches came together and blessed Edith and me. It was wonderful. When we got back to Las Vegas I told Edith that she was going to Memphis with me in November. I worked with Bishop Macklin every year but Edith had never been to Memphis. I assured her I would take care of everything well in advance because I wanted her to experience the 100th Year Centennial Celebration of the Church of God in Christ. The churches sponsored our trip. I called the Madison Hotel in Memphis, Tennessee and paid for our room. Then I called the travel agent and paid for both round trip airline tickets, so we were set to go.

The weekend before we were to leave for Memphis, I said to Edith, "Let's go to Los Angeles and do some shopping." We called the travel agent again, bought round-trip airplane tickets and rented a car for the day. We didn't take anything with us. When we arrived in the city, we each bought ourselves a new set of suitcases. I bought twelve new suits for myself and twelve new suits for Edith. While we waited for my suits to get tailored, we went shopping for shoes and accessories. We were really enjoying ourselves.

While we were shopping, we even saw other saints we knew from different parts of California shopping too. Edith and I had a great time. When we were finished, we had everything we needed for our trip. Everyone was going to be there this year. I had worked on the set up committee during the year and knew what we were in store for. My entire trip was paid for and we were ready to leave the following Sunday.

We arrived home from L.A. on Saturday night and I flew out again on Sunday morning to preach at the church in Reno. I was running late, so I ran through the airport in order not to miss my plane. As I ran, I felt a little pain in my left leg, but didn't think anything of it. I returned to Las Vegas late Monday night still excited about going to Memphis, but even more excited because my camera man from Sacramento was flying in on Tuesday morning. Since his schedule had started taking him out of the county a lot, I wanted him to train me and my sons on how to produce an entire show so we could do it ourselves.

I had just bought new equipment for my television ministry. My camera guy was prepared to set up the cameras and computers, as well as install all of the programs for me. I had just signed a contract with

Streaming Faith, and we were scheduled to air our Sunday and Tuesday night services live via internet after I returned from Memphis. This was a big part of my vision coming to pass. Streaming our services live would allow me to preach to all three churches at the same time. Finally things were looking up for me. After all of these years, I was happy about myself and my accomplishments. I couldn't have asked for more. My children were healthy and Edith and I were enjoying our journey together.

Chapter 11 Wrestling Lessons

Many times during your wrestle you will become weary, but no matter how weary you become, stay focused and never give up.

1. What are your skills, gifts, and talents? Your strengths? What are
    you particularly good at? Have you capitalized on these things? If
    not, why not? What positive changes can you make to play on your
    strengths?

    _____

    _____

    _____

    _____

    _____

2. Do you know who you are when you are going through difficult cir-
    cumstances? From where do you derive your self-identity: what you
    or others say about you, or what God says about you?

    _____

    _____

    _____

    _____

    _____

3. Write down your good points and your bad points. What can you do
    to strengthen your good points and improve on your bad points?

    _____

    _____

    _____

    _____

    _____

Chapter 11 Wrestling Strategies

1. Don't let yourself become overwhelmed by life:
    • Take time for yourself and your family.
    • Do not overload yourself with other people's work just because you know how to do it.

2. Don't take life so seriously.
    • Laugh.
    • Read good books.
    • See a good movie.
    • If need be, go to the park and swing on the swing.

3. Take your time to stop and smell the roses.
    • Enjoy your family and friends.
    • Love the Lord with all your heart.
    • Take a trip at least twice a year.

CHAPTER 1 2

A LIFE
CHANGING WOUND

*But he (Jesus) was wounded for our transgressions, he
was bruised for our iniquities, the chastisement of our peace was
upon Him; and with His stripes we are healed.* (Isaiah 53:5)

Tuesday, October 30, 2007 is a day I will never forget. I had a lot
to do before ten o'clock, the time I was to pick up my camera guy at the
airport. It started out like any other day. For the past five years I had been
working out at the gym two to three times a week. On this day, I woke up
and proceeded to do my normal routine. Edith and I went to the church
at six o'clock in the morning for prayer. When we arrived, I went out
the back door to turn the light off on our sign, when I found a homeless
young man sleeping right outside the door. He told me his story. I gave
him money for a hotel and asked him not to break in our gate again.
Edith and I prayed and then I took her to work.

The Break that Healed

When I arrived at the gym, I did my normal work out, starting
with the treadmill. Usually, after loosening up I was prepared for weight
lifting. But as I walked on the treadmill, my thigh began to hurt. I said
to myself, "No pain, no gain," and kept on walking. I wanted to increase
my speed, but since I was in pain, I only increased my pace.

As I ran, I suddenly heard my left leg crack. I didn't know what had
happened, but I fell to the floor and went into shock. The ambulance

came but I did not want to ride with them because of fear from stories I had heard. Instead, I phoned Edith and told her I had an accident and needed her to come take me to the hospital.

When she arrived at the gym, the paramedics were taking my blood pressure. They told me my leg wasn't broken but that I probably had pulled my ACL or tore a ligament. My blood pressure was 200/123; a normal pressure is 130/80. They insisted on driving me to the hospital. When I declined, they asked me to sign a release form stating that if anything happened to me on the way to the hospital, they would not be responsible.

When the two paramedics picked me up off the floor, my left leg just dangled and bounced around as I hopped on my right leg with my arms around their shoulders. The paramedics helped me get in my SUV as Edith held my leg for me. We arrived at the hospital at 6:45a.m. and Edith drove straight to the emergency room. She helped me get out of the car and into a wheelchair. I was in excruciating pain and could not control my leg; it kept falling. Edith held my left leg in place on top of my right foot as she pushed me in the wheelchair. The only way to relieve some of the pain was to hold my leg in a certain position, which was not working out very well.

Edith explained to the desk attendant what had happened and handed them the slip from the paramedics that stated how high my pressure was. They told her to push into the waiting area and wait for a nurse. Edith was very persistent and told them again what my blood pressure was. They told her again that we had to wait our turn.

Pain brings out the creative power that God placed in you.
-John Wynn

The waiting room was full of crying babies, people coughing, and other signs of pain and illness. They told us that they went in order by the most urgent need. People with breathing problems took precedence over people with injuries. When the nurse called me to take my vitals, Edith was determined to get someone to understand the seriousness of my condition. After she explained to the nurse how high my blood pressure was, the nurse said, "With your pressure this high you could have a stroke." They rushed me into the back, called the doctor in, and began working to get my blood pressure down.

Later, they sent me to radiology for x-rays of my leg. The x-ray technician called Edith back so she could help hold my leg still in order to get a good picture. The report came back that my left femur was definitely broken. I was admitted to the hospital and they began preparing me for surgery. They told Edith that the doctor was going to put a metal rod and some metal pins in my leg to put the bone back together and then put a cast on my leg. The nurses gave me medicine throughout the day to get my blood pressure down in order to perform the surgery. After waiting all day, the Internal Medicine doctor came in at 11:00 p.m. and told us they had postponed the surgery until 7:00a.m. the following morning because my blood pressure would not come down. She wanted to take more tests and ordered an ultrasound of my kidneys.

By the time the results were in, my mother and five of my sisters from Reno and Sacramento had arrived at the hospital. The doctor came in and told me that my high blood pressure had damaged my kidneys. I was heavily medicated both for the pain and the high blood pressure. The doctor told me that if I wanted to live I would have to start taking blood pressure medicine every day.

That blew my mind. Here I was, working out regularly for the past five years, losing weight, and trying to eat right so as to avoid taking medication, and in the end the *workout* caused me to have to take the medicine anyway. At the time, I did not understand what God was doing by allowing me to break my leg, but I know now that it was that break that literally saved my life. I came to realize that something much worse could have happened to me.

The next morning, my blood pressure was finally low enough to perform the surgery. As I lay in the preparation room, my life began to flash before me. I had never been admitted into the hospital before; I thought I was going to be in and out. Never before had I broken a bone or had any type of surgery. Anyone who knows me knows that I don't like hospitals.

I was in surgery for three hours. In the end, the doctor did not put in the rod or the pins, or put the cast on, as he had originally planned. Instead, he attached a 14-inch long metal plate to the outside of my femur, put in staples to close the incision, and covered everything with gauze and an ace bandage.

After the surgery I was so disoriented that I wanted to go home right away. I had lost so much blood during surgery that they had to give me a transfusion.

When my children arrived at the hospital later that day, my daughter Angel, who was nine at the time, told me that she had prayed for me. She said the Lord showed her the number five and told her that I would be going home on the fifth day. The Lord has always used Angel and has often given her visions that later came to pass. This was not unlike any other time. My children were so worried about me, that my daughters Farrah (13) and Angel (10) said they were not leaving the hospital until I did. Along with my wife, they stayed with me every night. I went home on Friday, which was indeed the fifth day. I praised God because He even increased my children's faith through my experience.

The Support of the Extended Family

The support we received from family and friends was wonderful, and I will be forever grateful to them and thankful to the Lord. Before I even made it home from the hospital, one of my pastor friends sent a FedEx package to my wife with $2,500.00 in it. Bishops and other Pastors sent money and well wishes. Edith received telephone calls from people all over the country, praying for me and asking about my well-being.

Family members and friends mailed get well cards with money enclosed. Pastors in both jurisdictions went out of their way to help my family. Some of my pastor and evangelist friends purchased airplane tickets and came personally to see about me. They stayed in my home, prayed for me and cooked for me. Some went with me to the doctor and helped me in and out of the car and to and from the wheelchair.

One pastor's wife called Edith and told her, "Don't do anything for Christmas Dinner except set the table. I am bringing your entire meal for Christmas." Several pastors visited me in the hospital, and some came to my house. The support we received was unbelievable. Sometimes you do so much for others that you don't think anyone cares about you. The Lord allowed me to see that people really loved and cared about me.

The Pain of Recovery

My recovery was the worst physical experience in my life! Due to the combination of the medications for pain and high blood pressure medication; I was shaking at night with sweat pouring down my face... and I was still racked with pain. I could not get any relief. This went on for two weeks. Edith transformed the entire family room into a recovery room, with a hospital bed and all, because I could not go up and down the stairs. Going to the bathroom was a nightmare because I could not bend my knee. Once, I overexerted myself and almost passed out in the bathroom. My oldest son, who was 16 at the time, had to help me to the bathroom and stand there and watch me to make sure I would not fall. Throughout my ordeal I cried often; it is possible to be so sick that it does not matter how old your aid is, you just want help.

When I went to the doctor two weeks later, he changed my prescription to something that he thought was better. I do not know what it was, but it was not better. The medication he gave me was called Percocet, and because it was a narcotic, it caused me to hallucinate. At one point I thought my oldest son was trying to kill me; that's how bad it was. My nerves were shot and I suffered from unpredictable and uncontrollable crying jags.

One night I was lying in the bed crying, and thinking I was going to lose my mind. I was trying to figure out what was going on with all the mixed messages in my head; feelings of confusion, frustration, and anger. I needed a word from the Lord. My spirit did not know what to grasp onto: God, or my pain medication. Everything that I knew changed; everything that I thought was was not.

As I lay there, the television was on and I was trying to find a remedy for my pain. I changed the channel to the Word Network and heard Norman Hutchins singing, "Lord, I want to dwell in Your presence; that's where I want to be."

After I heard these words, I began to worship God and became at peace within myself. My tears began to dry up, my mind became free, and I began to focus again upon the Word of the Lord. He spoke to me through His Word and reminded me that by His stripes I was healed. I kept on praying and I kept on focusing. The thought kept coming back to my mind, "Remember to say, 'I'm healed.'"

My dear brothers and sisters, it does not matter what your sickness is; mentally, physically or spiritually, you are healed. You have the victory! God is your friend! He'll walk with you and be by your side. Whatever you may be facing today in your life, the Bible asks,

> *"Is there anything too hard for God to do?"* (Genesis 18:14)

No, there is nothing too hard for the Lord to do. The Word of God lets us know that:

> *"The effectual fervent prayer of a righteous man availeth much."* (James 5:16b)

Remember also God's promise,

> *"I will never leave you nor forsake you."* (Hebrew 13:5b)

and Jesus said,

> *"Lo, I am with you always, even unto the end of the world."* (Mt. 28:20)

Chapter 12 Wrestling Lessons

These are things to remember when you're wounded:

1. In what ways do you take your health for granted? Do you have a
    concrete plan to guard your health through diet, exercise, and proper
    rest? If not, list three or four positive steps you will take immediately
    to create such a plan.

    _____

    _____

    _____

    _____

    _____

2. Have you ever been afflicted by people or by physical misfortunes?
    How did you handle the situation? Did you ever find peace within?
    How?

    _____

    _____

    _____

    _____

    _____

3. What effect has your sickness or misfortune had on your faith? How
    have your family and friends responded? Did these events expose your
    faith, friends and your true supporters?

    _____

    _____

    _____

    _____

    _____

Chapter 12 Wrestling Strategies

1. Take care of your mental and physical self.
    - Eat right.
    - Exercise.
    - Research medication given to you by doctors.

2. Get a check up regularly.
    - Know what's going on in your physical body.

3. When faced with adversity; keep your mind elevated through:
    - Prayer.
    - Bible reading.
    - Positive music.
    - Good books.
    - Inspirational movies.

4. Never give up, no matter what happens.

CHAPTER 13

THE UNDISPUTED CHAMPION

On Friday, December 7, 2007, I attended physical therapy for my fifth session. I felt absolutely no pain and was ready for my massage and ice. Usually, the light massage was given to me by either the office manager or another physical therapist. During this particular session, both of the regular men were occupied, so another man who was a licensed physical therapist gave me the massage.

As he began to massage my leg, I told him that my break was still healing. The closer he got to my break, the more nervous I became. I told him that it was hurting, but he said, "That's okay; it's good for you." I must have looked unconvinced, because he continued, "The only way I could break it is if I were to go down on it like this," which he demonstrated by hammering down on my leg with his elbow. I was in severe pain, but when he said it was good for me, I assumed it was normal pain. As he continued the massage, I heard cracking sounds, but he said it was just cartilage and scar tissue. I endured the pain as best I could until he was done. He put ice on my leg and then I went home.

Once home, I went straight to bed. I was still in extreme pain, but I kept hearing the guy say, "It's good for you." I crawled into bed and put my foot on a pillow. We examined my leg after I elevated it, and it was three times its normal size. Edith and one of my daughters looked at the side on my leg and touched it. My bone was right against my skin and they could feel the metal plate. A couple of minutes after I put my leg on the pillow, I moved it a tiny bit to adjust it, when we heard a loud "CRACK, CRACK, CRACK, CRACK, CRACK and I was instantly engulfed in EXCRUCIATING PAIN!! Still assuming that it was the cartilage and scar tissue as the physical therapist had said, I just put ice on it and took some Motrin. I thought it would feel better in the morning. The pain continued all night, and I kept taking Motrin and putting on fresh ice.

Pinned Down to Succeed

When I finally went back to the doctor's office, they took more x-rays and found out that my leg was broken again. All I could do was cry. It was unbelievable because I had been healing so well and was making so much progress. The doctor explained that he needed to take out the metal plate, staple that incision, make two more incisions, one at the top of my leg and the other just above my knee, and then insert a metal rod 13 inches long and screw it to my bone. On December 11th at 7:30pm, they took me into the pre-surgery waiting room. I went into the operating room at 7:45pm and came out around 10:30pm. The doctor said that the surgery had gone better than he expected and that my leg was going to be stronger now with the rod in.

I did not understand why all this was happening, so when I came out of surgery I asked God, "Why did you allow my leg to break a second time?" I sensed a presence on the left side on my hospital bed and heard these words: "The first surgery was for your vital organs and this surgery was for your leg." I thought about the first surgery and said to myself, "If I had not lost so much blood or if my blood pressure had not been so high; I might not be alive today." After the second surgery I became more thankful and more appreciative of how much God really did care for me.

Sometimes God allows us to go through trials and tribulations, and experience a breaking in our flesh or our spirit because He knows that sometimes His people choose wrestling matches they cannot win. In my case, I encountered a ten-year wrestle that I did not realize I was engaged in. I had worked myself to the point where I tried to ignore my pain and the wrestle. I kept doing the work of God in spite of the pain; I guess I got used to it. It was so familiar to me that I never recognize it was a problem.

While I was flat on my back, everything came full circle. On January 5, 2008 I asked my son to find a notebook to write in because I wanted to journal information about our new webcast that was going to launch in about one hour. He went into the office and found one of my old journals. I asked to see it before he started writing in it. I opened the journal, and there in my own hand writing were words I had written exactly ten years earlier to the very day. My son had found this journal by accident. For 10 years it had sat unnoticed and unused on my bookshelf.

As I read the thoughts of my past and began to reflect on my present at the same time, I found a code in my writing that answered so many of my questions. I received the answers for my current situation that began to solve the problems through writing this book. I also discovered why I was the pastor of three churches simultaneously.

Wrestling Venues:

Greater Harvest Church, Sacramento

I realize now that the Sacramento church was a training camp for me. Some of the members felt that I had abandoned them when I moved to Las Vegas with my family. However, moving to Vegas was necessary for the fulfillment of God's plan. Sacramento was a place for me to learn to build leaders and train people to do Kingdom work. Six of the men who worked under my ministry in the Sacramento church, are now pastors themselves, using the wisdom and teaching that God allowed me to impart into them. It also developed me as a leader because I connected with Bishop Macklin who gave me great insight on how to be an effective leader. Through the struggles of having to relocate repeatedly, losing members, dealing with family in ministry and my own family's stability, I learned how to help other pastors who are dealing with the same or similar issues. I am able to encourage them not to give up and to be resilient and faithful in their assignment.

Greater Harvest Church, Las Vegas

The church in Las Vegas was to develop my children. I explained a few chapters back that I often overlooked my children's talents because I already had talented people working in the ministry. After relocating to Vegas, God allowed me to go through a time where I did not have anybody there who knew how to do what was being done in Sacramento. I had to train my children how to play the instruments, sing, teach, witness, pray, and be faithful to their ministry. It also gave me confidence to work in the community and provided me business opportunities that blessed my family and others. I was able to train people for jobs through our Community Development Program, open a childcare center, and partner up with the Clark County Unified School District's Adult Education Department. Most of all, through the experience of breaking my leg, my family became very close and they have been and remain my biggest supporters to this day.

Greater Harvest Church, Reno

The Reno church served as an inheritance of my father, the Late Rev. Willie J. Wynn, who was the first African-American on the Governor's cabinet in the State of Nevada in the sixties, and my brother-in-law, Pastor Live Tau, who served for fifteen years, who acquired property and maintained the church. Reno also taught me stability. I learned how to deal with mature saints (most of the mature saints are sixty years of age and above). I developed patience in my decision-making, church democracy, learning how to get a consensus from the church as well as from my head deacon, who has been with the church for forty-five years. This church showed me what consistent church members look like. Some of these members have remained faithful for twenty-five plus years and are yet working in the ministry. Their unwavering faith and support to the church has been a blessing to many, including and especially me, even when others left.

After the Wrestle

It was January 5, 2008, twenty-five days after my second surgery. After I read my journal, I went to church for the first time and preached to the world live through Streaming Faith on the internet. My message was, "You Can't Kill My Dream!" That was the day I thought I was finished writing this book. After a long 10-year wrestle, I was finally able to bring closure and it felt great!

Two months later, in March 2008, I aired my first world-wide television broadcast to 140 countries; 50 million homes on The Word Network. I also recorded my first spoken word music CD, titled "Perspective." The title of the first song on the album is "Be Healed." I had a big CD release party on September 20, 2008 at the Alexis Park Hotel in Las Vegas. My entire family attended as well as many friends and members of all three of my churches. God was opening doors and my journey became very interesting indeed. Some said that I had done more work in ministry after I broke my leg than I had in the entire 16 years I'd been a pastor. What they do not understand is, after my encounter with God, I received clear instructions for my future.

When I started writing this book, I thought the title was going to be "Will you be made whole?" I did not learn until writing this chapter that not only was I being healed physically, but emotionally and spiritually as well. After ten years of being hurt, the Lord allowed me to be made whole and then He told me the title of this book was to be *Wrestling with god*. It was then that I realized that I had lost the wrestling match with Almighty God. I was pinned me to the mat and I was down for the count: "1…2…3… You're out; and then I was out! All I could say was, "Yes, Lord!"

Chapter 13 Wrestling Lessons

God is the ultimate champion, and no matter what you face or go through, know that *"all things work together for good to them that love God, to them who are the called according to his purpose."* (Romans 8:28)

1. In what ways has God shown himself to be your Champion? Be specific with your answer. Do you define your success based on someone else's appearance?

_____

_____

_____

_____

_____

2. Briefly describe the last time you felt so discouraged that you were ready to give up. How did you resolve the situation? Write down the names of every person (if any) who helped you through that time. If you have not already done so, take time to thank them in some way. Do you allow your circumstances to make you want to give up?

_____

_____

_____

_____

3. In what ways do you show that you are faithful and committed to your purpose?

_____

_____

_____

_____

Chapter 13 Wrestling Strategies

1. Stick to your plans.
    - Bad things happen to good people, so when things happen, just do what works for you and you will succeed.
    - Stay focused on the plan.
    - Work your plan.

2. No one can beat you being you.
    - To thy own self be true.
    - Discover the greatness in you.

3. Fulfill what God has given you to do in:
    - Business.
    - Ministry.
    - Family.
    - Relationships.

4. Try to minimize your weaknesses and maximize your strengths. Focus on your talents.

CHAPTER 14

LEAVING THE WRESTLING RING

Humble yourselves therefore under the mighty hand of God, that he may exalt you in due time: Casting all your care upon him; for he careth for you. Be sober, be vigilant; because your adversary the devil, as a roaring lion, walketh about, seeking whom he may devour: Whom resist stedfast in the faith, knowing that the same afflictions are accomplished in your brethren that are in the world. But the God of all grace, who hath called us unto his eternal glory by Christ Jesus, after that ye have suffered a while, make you perfect, stablish, strengthen, settle you. To him be glory and domin-ion forever and ever. Amen. (1 Peter 5:6-11)

When I overcame the little gods in my subconscious mind and I realized I was not wrestling with the Almighty God, I knew that I was no match for the King of Kings and the Lord of Lords. I discovered that my wrestle all those years was because I felt that God had turned His back on me and was blessing everyone else, but leaving me out. Then God began speaking to me, saying, "You have been in My way. I wanted to bless you years ago, but you were focused more on the church buildings and the members then you were on Me. I will never allow My glory to be substituted for earthly goods."

After the Lord spoke to me, I thought about the time when I saw my mother faced with a dilemma because of my stepfather. She was so upset about what he had said to her that she was shaking. I ran to my mother and became upset with God for allowing that to happen. My mother told me, "When you are hurt, never take out your frustration on God. Always pray in the will of God, so that when things don't go your way, you will not be upset." It was clear that God was allowing me to walk out of the wrestling ring and allowing me to embrace my future with vision and hope.

I walked away from life-changing matches with wrestling lessons, wrestling strategies and life experiences that will change the lives of God's people all over the world. When I came to myself, I realized that my wrestle was not to stop the vision that was in me, but to bring the vision to pass. Since I have left the wrestling ring the Lord has blessed me with the desires of my heart. The following are only a few of my Praise Reports, just to bring you up to date:

God gets the Glory and I got the Victory!

1. In January, 2009, I released the church in Sacramento, founded in 1995, and appointed Pastor James Allen.

2. In January, 2009, I released Pastor Eric Barnes; my Assistant for 15 years, to start a church. He now has a great church in Long Beach, California.

3. On September 18, 2009, I was elevated to the office of Presiding Bishop of International Church Fellowship, Inc.

4. In November, 2009, I started a film production company and wrote my first screenplay.

5. On July 8, 2010, I released the church in Las Vegas and relocated my family to Reno, Nevada. For the first time in 11 years, I am the pastor of one church in one location.

6. On March 23, 2011, I was inducted into the Joint College of African-American Bishops under His Grace, Bishop J. Delano Ellis and received Apostolic Succession.

7. On March 23, 2011, I also received my Degree of Doctor of Divinity in Cleveland, Ohio.

8. On April 1, 2011, The City of Reno's Plan Examiner approved our plans to build our new church facility in Reno. The design is the same church I wanted to build in Sacramento years ago. The new two-story educational wing will be named in honor of the founder; my father, "The Reverend Willie J. Wynn Educational Facilities."

9. In September 2011, I wrote a curriculum and developed a mentoring program called Youth Empowered to Succeed (Y.E.S.) and partnered up with the 25th largest school district in the Nation, Washoe County School District.

10. In October 2011, I became a Chaplain for the City of Reno Police Department.

All my wrestling with the little gods was just for Almighty God to show me that it's not about working for myself but to keep Him in the center of my life. If I do, He will never let me down. This is just the beginning, because *greatness knows no limits.*

The Lord spoke to me and said, "It doesn't matter how much money you have, how big or small your congregation may be, how large your home is, how many businesses you have, or how much property you have obtained; it's all about being in My will."

> *Many will say to me in that day, Lord, Lord, have we not prophesied in thy name? and in thy name have cast out devils? and in thy name done many wonderful works? And then will I profess unto them, I never knew you: depart from me, ye that work iniquity. Therefore whosoever heareth these sayings of mine, and doeth them, I will liken him unto a wise man, which built his house upon a rock: And the rain descended, and the floods came, and the winds blew, and*

beat upon that house; and it fell not: for it was founded upon a rock. (Matthew 7:22-25)

It wasn't until after I broke my femur that I came to myself. I now know what the will of God is for my life; to be faithful to Him unto death!

ABOUT THE AUTHOR

DR. JOHN WYNN

Born and reared in Reno, Nevada, Dr. John Wynn is a successful entrepreneur who has achieved many of his goals early in life. At the age of twenty six he began to air his own television show titled, "Set Free" on a local cable station. The show encouraged people throughout Northern California for over eight years. By the age of thirty, his first book: NEW LEVELS, NEW D.E.V.I.L.S, was a complete sellout. At the age of thirty five, he was the founder and president of New Levels Community Development Center; which included a childcare center and an adult educational facility to benefit low-income families in Las Vegas, Nevada. He also founded Wynn-Win Enterprises, LLC; a record label he created to produce Christian inspirational music, which includes his own spoken word music CD titled "Perspective."

In January 2008, he expanded his ten year television ministry when he launched his international show on DIRECTV's Word Network Channel which has aired in 144 countries around the world. As an accomplished author and musician, he has produced three inspirational music CD's and written two noteworthy books. Additionally, he established Wynn Film Productions, LLC, a film production company which currently has four spectacular movies ready for production. In September 2009, at the age of thirty nine, he was consecrated as bishop and became Chief Apostle and Presiding Bishop of International Church Fellowship, Inc. In March 2011, he received Apostolic Succession and was inducted into the Joint College of African American Bishops in Cleveland, Ohio. That same year, he received his Doctrine of Divinity.

He currently offers his educational program in six schools of the Washoe County School District in Reno, Nevada. The program is titled, Youth Empowered to Succeed (Y.E.S. Program). Through his initiative and persistence, he developed a curriculum with an accompanying supplemental workbook that garners positive behavioral results for student participants. His program has been endorsed and supported by the Mayor of the City of Reno, the Chief of Police, the Superintendent of Washoe County School District, various local educators including site administrators and counselors.

Today, he is a rising, stellar community leader who has received countless support from city officials, politicians and community activists. He supports the local education system with a major focus on student self-development and individual responsibility. He is a member of the Education Alliance of Washoe County School District and a committee member of the Child Welfare Network in Las Vegas, Nevada. He is also the Co-Chairman of AACCONN (African American Clergy Council of Northern Nevada) which consists of twenty two pastors from local churches throughout Northern Nevada. In addition to his many responsibilities, he serves as Chaplain for the Reno Police Department.

As an accomplished lecturer, he has been the invited keynote speaker and presenter for various organizations and corporations both local and internationally. His most memorable occasion is being a viable member on a panel for PBS radio and contributing to the topic of "Evils of the World." He is honored by the opportunity to give the invocation for the IACLEA (International Association of Campus Law Enforcement), the NAACP, the Reno Police Department and countless other organizations. He continues to speak across the world, effectively transcending racial and cultural barriers. His appearances on international television, national radio, and online internet streaming for nearly two decades are unparalleled.

eGenco

Generation Culture Transformation
Specializing in publishing for generation culture change

Visit us Online at:
www.egen.co
www.goingebook.com

Write to: eGen Co. LLC
824 Tallow Hill Road
Chambersburg, PA 17202 USA
Phone: 717-461-3436
Email: info@egen.co

 facebook.com/egenbooks

 youtube.com/egenpub

 egen.co/blog